Psychotherapy and Religion

The Author: Henry Guntrip is psychotherapist on the staff of the Department of Psychiatry at Leeds University, England. He was for eighteen years a Congregational minister to two parish churches. He lectured for four years at a theological college on pastoral psychology, and practiced psychotherapy five years while still a pastor.

No. 7535A

Henry
Guntrip

PSYCHOTHERAPY

AND

RELIGION

with a foreword by

Rollo May

HARPER & BROTHERS *publishers* NEW YORK

Contents

Foreword

by ROLLO MAY

THE most crucial issue in contemporary psychotherapy, in my judgment, is whether the aim is to help the person gain *freedom from anxiety* or rather to help him confront anxiety experiences with the aim of *enlarging his freedom*. In the former view, anxiety and conflict—what Dr. Guntrip calls 'mental pain'—are seen as neurotic and evil in themselves, experiences one should avoid at all costs, something to gain *relief* from in therapy. In the latter view, on the other hand, conflict and anxiety are seen as the inescapable concomitants of any human being's struggle toward authentic selfhood and fulfillment of his potentialities for creative interreaction with his world.

This dilemma is not only of decisive importance for therapy, but it is an expression of a basic polarity in our culture as well. On the first side fall the 'peace of mind' and 'confident living' emphases, in which a placid type of inner harmony is the goal, and conformity to the social standards of success and following the will of God are the same thing. On this side falls the kind of psychology which emphasizes adjustment; the kind of psychiatry which sees tranquillity, comfort, and absence of conflict as the goals; and the kind of psychoanalysis which assumes that libinal satisfaction and release from tension are the ultimate criteria of healthy personality.

And, speaking in broader social terms, on this side of the issue falls the great and growing dependence on the tranquillizing drugs and sedatives, not to mention alcohol, as methods of relief from everyday conflict as well as neurotic anxiety. In a recent article entitled, 'Why So Many Ministers Break Down,' *Life* magazine quoted the statement of one clergyman to the effect that the only way he could get along under the pressure of his work and the heavy demands on his time was to take the tranquillizing drugs. This remark would be singular and only mildly pathetic if it did not represent such a widespread attitude and practice in our day with respect to personal conflicts. And it should be added, when people artificially remove the motivating power of their anxiety and conflict, they tend to rely on equally heavy doses of benzedrene and other stimulants to whip themselves into action; and a vicious circle is begun. The reason for this circle is not centrally the heavy pressure that everyone seems to be under in our highly driven society. Rather, the reason, if I may be so grandiloquent as to phrase it this way, is a basic flaw in our idea of man. We make ourselves over in the image of our machines. Drug companies now advertise certain pills as 'specifics' for anxiety, apparently totally unaware that anxiety is never specific, but is always the symptom of some problem that cries for correction in our relation to ourselves and our world. And if, as in the case of our unfortunate clergyman, the pill gets him over the symptom of anxiety without his needing to solve the underlying problem, he may well have lost his best guide and source of motivating power to confront the real conflict, namely why he compulsively overworks in the first place.

On the other side of this basic issue fall the therapies—and I do not believe they can, like the proverbial sheep and goats, be separated into schools—which hold that man's future is such that he can achieve emotional health only as he is continually in the process of *becoming*. That is to say, harmony and comfort are not the goals of life; rather, the goal is the expansion and heightening of consciousness, and the development of ethical responsibility and those other unique human potentialities which go with heightened consciousness.

On this side, too, fall Kierkegaard's marvelously penetrating psychological analyses of the human self. 'The self is a conscious synthesis,' he writes, 'of infinitude and finitude which relates itself to itself, *whose task is to become itself.*' Kierkegaard continually proclaims that to venture in life causes anxiety, but not to venture is to lose oneself. 'For if I have ventured amiss—very well, then life helps me by its pun-

ishment. But if I have not ventured at all—who then helps me?
And, moreover, if by not venturing at all in the highest sense
(and to venture in the highest sense is precisely to become
conscious of oneself) I have gained all earthly advantages . . .
and lose my self! What of that?'

Paul Tillich's profound analyses likewise illustrate this
second side. For anxiety must be confronted in its *normal* as
well as neurotic forms, holds Tillich, and every person must
take upon himself the normal anxiety of finiteness (death),
meaninglessness and guilt if he is to experience the 'courage
to be.'

The point of first significance which struck me in reading
Dr. Gunstrip's book was the clarity with which he sees this
basic issue. Though he would no doubt not analyze it exactly
as I do, there is no vagueness about where he stands. He
tellingly points out how people in our society prefer physical
to mental pain, and how it is all too human to use physical
ailments as substitutes for and ways of avoiding the much
more difficult and perplexing task of confronting one's
anxiety. For by this means one is able to avoid the burden of
consciousness; 'It is not *I* who am ill, but my body,' and one
gives himself over to the potion which may bring relief.
Dostoevski decades ago described in dramatic scenes the price
of this tendency: to give up the burden of consciousness is
also to give up one's freedom.

Guntrip is well aware, however, that admitting the inescapable and constructive aspects of anxiety and conflict does
not at all mean 'rationalizing' neurosis and suffering. Neurotic
—or as Tillich puts it, pathological—anxiety is to be over-
come, by means of understanding and psychotherapy. But
we can best accomplish this by facing the fact that though
anxiety and mental suffering are evil, they are not the worst
evils in the world; there is one greater evil—to be so anxious
to avoid conflict that one loses one's chance for new psychological and spiritual growth.

Dr. Guntrip presents a penetrating discussion of how neurotic problems begin, what situations keep the child from developing as a person in his own right, and how the neurotic mechanisms are perpetuated. All his writing is infused with concern for the human being as a *person,* but he avoids the tendencies toward superficiality which sometimes go along with the emphases of the interpersonal schools. He retains the powerful concepts of unconscious dynamics, though in much broader form than the orthodox Freudian. He believes that the questions of values and religion must be an integral part of any psychoanalytic discussion which pretends to deal with the whole living person.

The keen analyses in this book will speak for themselves. I should like only to underline two other points of special value. First, it is good to have Guntrip's presentation of the viewpoint of his colleague and teacher, W. R. D. Fairbairn, whose psychoanalytic studies are not well known in this country. Fairbairn apparently makes the *unconscious personal.* That is to say, he keeps the concept of unconscious motivation, but he holds that these motivations themselves partake of the personal qualities of all human existence; hence it is faulty to understand the unconscious by the limited model of mechanical determinism.

And finally let me underline Dr. Guntrip's highly interesting and in some ways original discussion of schizoid personalities. The schizoid character—the type of person who is alienated, aloof, lonely, detached—is becoming almost the norm in our technological society. These are people who long for love but are convinced it is unattainable, and who are afraid of the very power of their own longings. Dr. Guntrip's contribution to understanding this character type which is so complex and so common will be especially welcomed.

This thoughtful book, broad and humane without sacrificing intellectual integrity, is the kind of writing needed for intelligent laymen as well as professional persons in the field of the science of man today.

Introduction

THIS little book has grown out of a lecture given in 1951 at an Easter School for Old Students of New College, London. I was privileged to take part as an old student of the College and also because I was invited to read a paper on the somewhat vague, if broad, title, 'Guiding the Perplexed'. The general subject under discussion was 'The Holy Spirit', and papers were read on the Old Testament and New Testament teaching, the teaching of Congregationalism, and the theological problems concerning the Holy Spirit. My task was to bring up the rear with an attempt to relate the subject to the painful realities of contemporary living.

I own to having felt some apprehension as to whether my contribution would fit into the general scheme of things. My task was to speak about the actual troubles experienced by perplexed individuals and what could be done to help mentally tormented persons. It is not easy to lead a group from the lofty heights of sacred history and theological exploration down into the valley of the shadow of human misery and illness, depression and disease, fearful failure and frightening fantasy. I presumed that I was invited to speak as a psychotherapist, out of my experience of seeking to help individuals with broken personalities which needed mending. I knew only too well that 'the perplexed' were not a self-contained class apart. We are all perplexed, we are all at various times and in varying degrees unhappy, anxious, and rather nearer than we care to think to some breaking point in faith, or in mental or bodily fitness. The psychotherapist has his own personal experience of the suffering he sees in his patients. When he speaks publicly his subject-matter agitates things in the minds of his hearers which they do not want to have stirred up. The psychotherapist is well used to being met with a curious double attitude of mixed eagerness and hostility.

The discussion of Biblical, ecclesiastical and theological teaching on an intellectual level does not necessarily stir up anxiety as such, unless at some point there comes a sharp challenge to our own pet ideas, which have for us a much greater defensive and security value than we recognize. Among its wider values, our faith must of necessity be a major bulwark against our fears so that when it is challenged by new ideas we are apt to defend it with a heat born of anxiety. But the discussion of common human ills, emotional and physical, and of the subject matter of psychotherapy, leads us at once to the borderland between mental security and insecurity. Here we are all capable of experiencing far more anxiety than is comfortable to endure. It is my experience that audiences react to lectures on such subjects either with a defensive hostility or else with a marked eagerness to know more and go further. I am bound to say that usually the majority are responsive, provided psychiatric material is not presented with unbecoming dogmatism. They recognize that the patient analysis of the hidden workings of the human mind, which is being carried on by the competent trained psychoanalyst and psychotherapist is bringing to light knowledge of momentous and far-reaching importance. Nevertheless such subjects are never dealt with except to the accompaniment of some arousal of varying degrees of anxiety in the individuals composing the audience.

To me it was a gratifying experience to find that my contribution could be assimilated by the scheme of the conference in a helpful way. It was beneficial to have some private conversation beforehand with Dr. Geoffrey F. Nuttall and Dr. A. R. Vine, whose questions, comments and sometimes doubts helped me to relate my material better to the needs of the conference. My own eighteen years of experience in the active ministry in two churches enabled me to understand readily their points of view. The lecture has now been expanded into book form as a result of a wish expressed by the late

Dr. Sydney Cave to see the material made available by publication. He had kindly promised to consider writing a Foreword, and it is a matter of deep regret to me that he passed away before there was an opportunity to show him the finished MS.

The psychologist must say what he knows, remembering, with befitting humility, that much more scientific research in his field lies hidden in the years to come, and that his theory must therefore be tentative. Science has no place for dogmatic finality. On the other hand, though theoretical explanations will vary, real facts are being discovered and facts are capable of shining by their own light through the shifting mists of hypothesis. The theologian and philosopher must not turn a blind eye to the psychologist's facts because they may be disturbing to his own theories. He must seek to understand their meaning in the wider contexts in which he wishes to see them. Yet in the end, this book seeks not merely to offer some factual grist to the theological mill, but even more to offer useful knowledge to the working pastor. The pastor is often in fact liable to severe discouragement because so many human problems prove to be most intractable of solution; and human nature, in spite of much worship, preaching and devoted ministry, and, we may add, psychotherapy, changes so very little. To see clearly how and why human nature *is* so hard to change, should at least save us from the facile optimism that only ends in deeper discouragement, and it may strengthen our resolve to go on working at the difficult problem. It is my hope that this small book may at least cast some light of understanding on complex problems so that the pastor may be able to see a bit more clearly what is the inner nature of the human troubles with which he deals. If I have not been able to provide a kind of psychological 'ready reckoner' in which the answers to a multitude of particular problems could be quickly looked up, I may have been able to show something of the light thrown by 'dynamic psychology' on that difficult task, the understanding of human nature.

NOTE: *The term "mental pain" as used throughout the text has been rendered "anxiety" in the chapter headings of this edition.*

Part I.
ANXIETY

CHAPTER I

Anxiety and Resistance to Mental Healing

THE minister as preacher has a message to declare and a teaching
to expound. The minister as pastor has troubled individual
men and women to understand and help. It is possible to hide
behind a smoke-screen of words in preaching, especially if
one has a glib tongue. The congregation of the faithful who
attend regularly are not over critical of sermons, and provided
the preacher is moderately interesting or stimulating he may
'get by' with no great depth of understanding or profundity
of thought. He may even do well enough by echoing the
prejudices of his hearers, and reaffirming the sanctified traditional 'good words' upon which their faith rests. By and large
the majority of a congregation are regular Church goers and
do not come specifically and urgently needing some particular kind of help. There is always liable to be the troubled
individual, who has come into the service for worship with
some definite burden on his mind. Even so he can appreciate
the fact that the preacher is not omniscient, has other people
to preach to besides him, and that the majority of the congregation have probably no clear-cut and definite problem in
mind. If he does not find anything in the sermon to help him,
he may pluck up courage to go and see the preacher after the
service in the vestry. If something in the sermon has helped
him, he may perhaps be all the more likely to seek a private
interview. In that case we must hope he will not have the
experience of one young man who did screw up his courage
to go to the vestry after service to lay a very big problem
before a very famous preacher. In his own words: 'The great
man was obviously anxious to get home to his supper and cut
short my halting statement with a few encouraging platitudes

and the assurance that "things would work out all right". I left feeling let down and in despair. I could not talk of my problem at home, and knew no one else who seemed likely to understand.'

It is possible to 'get by' in preaching. It is quite impossible to 'get by' when you are face to face with an individual human being in real difficulties. Either you *can help* or you *cannot*. If you do not know anything effective to say or do, then you will do more harm than good by attempting any sort of encouraging bluff. It is better to be sympathetically frank and say 'I do not know how to help or advise you, but you need help and we must find someone else who can meet your need.' It was said of a once noted preacher that if any individual sought a private interview to lay some problem before him, his invariable reply was: 'I'll preach about that next Sunday.' But neither can one 'get by' by using preaching as an illegitimate escape from the responsibility of a personal ministry. The most searching test for the minister will be found on the pastoral and personal side of his work. This test can only be escaped by being the kind of man whom it is so obviously useless to approach with personal problems that no one ever thinks of coming to you. Perhaps the most spurious form of ministry is that in which the glitter of public success masks an inability to make helpful and healing contact with individuals. The immortal moments in the story of the Gospel are not the public utterances of Jesus, but His intimate personal conversations with such as Nicodemus, the woman at the well in Samaria, the man whose name was Legion, and Mary Magdalene.

It is the ministry to the troubled individual that concerns us here. At the outset one overriding fact must be made clear. The troubled individual is *in pain*. He is suffering from pain in his mind. He is not unlikely to be suffering from pain—or at least considerable and fluctuating discomfort—in body as well, for any mental disturbance rapidly upsets the smooth and orderly working of our physical organism. Anxious people feel vaguely bodily unwell even when they have no definite physical symptoms. But mental pain must always be present.

It is generally agreed that the results of the scientific study of human nature ought to be accepted and used by religiously minded people, just as much when they accrue from the study of the mind, as when they accrue from the study of the body. We do not regard it as evidence of great spirituality to refuse an injection of penicillin for streptococcal infection and rely solely on prayer. There is no more reason on religious grounds to reject a psychotherapeutic analysis of a morbid anxiety state and exhort only to religious exercises. Science and religion, understanding and love, must work together. It was the writer's experience in 1950 to broadcast some talks on 'Nerves' and it was gratifying to find that out of over 1,500 letters from listeners, only six attacked 'all this modern psychological nonsense' with the plea 'Let's get back to the real gospel'.

We do not today set science and religion in necessary antagonism, and we need to call upon the full resources of psychological science if we are to understand and deal rightly with this tremendous fact of *mental pain*. This cannot be done by trying to give glib and simple remedies, or snappy bits of semi-psychological advice. That would be unworthy of the gravity of this vast problem of human pain and puzzlement. It can only be done by trying to open up the grim challenging realities of the human situation, and in going along this realistic path we must have the courage to put aside easy solutions. Only by admitting that we are often helpless to relieve human suffering because we are too ignorant about it, only by refusing to make religion a convenient dumping ground of unsolved problems, and only by believing that God calls us to fearless and patient investigation, can we slowly but surely bring any real help and guidance to the suffering and the perplexed.

The title suggested for the original lecture was 'Guiding the Perplexed'. That, however, is inadequate. It lifts human troubles too much on to the intellectual plane. It suggests that helpful explanations to puzzled minds, and, perhaps, that theological enlightenment for credal doubts, is what is most needed. One of the first things one discovers in psychotherapy is that intellectual explanation is of astonishingly small practical value. It makes no decisive difference to the basic structure of the personality. Intellectual explanation only clears up intellectual difficulties of the kind which can be cleared up by lucid explanation. If a person does not rightly understand some doctrine, intellectual explanations can clear away his mental fog. But the more intractable intellectual problems, the stubborn doubts on matters of basic importance, do not yield to such treatment. They have their roots in, and mask, emotional problems, and very likely are manifestations of the total set-up of the doubter's (or believer's) personality. People of strongly held but opposed beliefs never succeed in resolving their differences by purely intellectual explanation, criticism and discussion. Beliefs are one of our major systems of defence against the internal and external arousal of anxiety, and both our beliefs and our doubts have behind them deep, invisible needs of our total self. If we allow our beliefs to be undermined by an opponent, we are liable to become a prey to fears.

The fundamental human problems do not lie in the region of the intellect. They lie in the region of our personal needs and our emotional relationships and they concern our basic satisfactions, fulfilments and frustrations in living. We shall be closer to the heart of the human problem if we think not of 'Guiding the Perplexed' but of 'Succouring the Unloved'. What we need to know is how to remedy the ravages in human nature due to deprivation of love.

Intellectual explanation, however, even when it bears on the real human problems, is still useless in itself. One of the traps that the inexperienced psychotherapist falls into is that of explaining too much, and too soon, to the patient, instead of helping the patient, by listening, to work through his own problems himself and grow their solution on the dynamic level of feeling and impulse. Psychotherapy can be blocked by allowing it to become an intellectual discussion of a person's difficulties or an attempt to enlighten, teach or indoctrinate him. May be purely intellectual, educational, preaching can block a congregation emotionally for worship. There is a great difference between lecturing and preaching, and the difference is primarily in the more impersonal nature of the communication of information over against the intensely personal nature of devotion and worship.

We must not, of course, deny the importance of clear thinking and intellectual understanding. We can get nowhere without it, but it is a means to an end. Understanding is a utilitarian method which aims at promoting use and enjoyment. The art of the psychoanalyst lies not in interpreting and explaining everything the patient says. That could amount simply to a disintegrating breakdown of his mental organization. It would also constitute such a perpetual interference with the patient's own mental processes that their natural development and unfolding would be rendered impossible. *The psychoanalyst rather watches the progress of significant developments towards self-discovery, insight and confidence as the patient talks, and, just at the right time makes just the right kind of observation* to help the patient to see more clearly what he himself is really feeling, though not recognizing, all the time. *Psychoanalytical interpretations aim not at giving the patient an intellectual understanding of his problems, but at helping him to experience with full conscious awareness his own inner self and life.*

This is very different from many popular notions of how psychotherapy works. There seems to be some necessity to voice a warning against naïvete and simple mindedness about psychotherapy, for it is apparently all too easy for some credulous enthusiasts to think that a bit of psychological knowledge can be applied by rule of thumb and may be relied on automatically to produce a sudden and miraculous cure. A patient once brought to me a letter she had received from a minister of religion from whom she had been receiving 'psychological treatment'. The letter stated: 'Nervous trouble is frequently traceable to some episode of childhood.' A list of cases was then given in which quite extensive neurotic symptoms were described, each followed by such a comment as: 'I traced it to an operation at the age of four which frightened him', or 'Traced to a childhood occasion of sleeping alone in an attic which frightend her', or 'Traced to his being laughed at his first day at school'. The list ended with the statement, 'all these came to a complete recovery'.

That, of course, is complete nonsense. If every human being who had on some occasion experienced some fright in childhood was thereby doomed to adult neurosis, the entire human race would almost certainly be in a state of mental breakdown. Moreover, if neurosis could be so easily and quickly cured as this pretentious letter stated, psychotherapy would be no more than an interesting trick of detective work. The long and painful psychoanalytical treatments required to produce really thoroughgoing changes in personality would be quite incomprehensible. The deep seated mental pains from which many people suffer cannot be relieved by neat little devices of psychological explanation. There is no quick and easy magic, but only blood and toil and sweat and tears, along the psychotherapeutic pathway.

It is well to remember that one cannot become a psychotherapist merely by some intellectual grasp of the theory of psychoanalysis gained from the study of a list of recommended books. It is quite possible to master the theory without developing any genuine insight into human nature, human motives, and the sources of mental pain face to face with *actual individuals*. The mere theorist may be quite helpless when confronted with this or that particular person with all his subtle and complex defences against anxiety. The eager enthusiast for psychotherapy would do well to remember that, since people who are in emotional difficulties can only win through to a genuine solution by recognizing the source of their difficulties inside themselves, they are often anything but grateful at first for the really appropriate kind of help. Some types will become more hostile—because more anxious —the closer you get to the real causes of their trouble. If you try to force them to see something they are not yet capable of admitting without too grave an outbreak of anxiety, they will either ignore or repudiate what you say, or else they will hate you. The unskilled psychotherapist who tries to give insight too quickly usually antagonizes his patient.

Psychotherapy is apt to appeal to some minds with all the glamour of 'the latest thing' in scientific progress, a wonderful new found pill to cure all ills. Many ministers think they would like to take up psychotherapy with but little realization of what it involves. It is not in this mental atmosphere that the skill, tact and insight are acquired to lay bare in a healing way the wounded and painful areas in the mental life of men and women.

I am asking and seeking to answer the question 'Does the knowledge and experience gained by the psychotherapist throw any light on human nature and human problems of a kind that is valuable for its bearings on religious ministry?' I hope to show that it does. For the moment we may take 'the perplexed and suffering' to mean all human beings who are in any kind of personal trouble that might lead them to seek help from a minister of religion or a professional psychotherapist. A considerable number of patients who come ultimately to a psychotherapist have made previous attempts to talk out their problems with ministers of religion, and general medical practioners. Sometimes, it is clear, they were fortunate enough to find a doctor or minister who possessed real human sympathy, and much sound common sense and intuitive understanding of human nature; and they received real help for the time being, if only of a supportive rather than a radically curative kind. In other cases they have fallen into the hands of a doctor or minister who lacked real insight and have come away, either feeling that they were odd, queer, and no one could understand them, or else that it was all somehow their own fault and other people blamed and looked down on them as weak and selfish.

I have elsewhere (in *Psychology for Ministers and Social Workers*, 1949, Second Edition 1953) expressed my conviction that there is a social and pastoral psychology which is invaluable for those who are in any vocational position to help their fellow men, even though it should be kept distinct from full scale psychotherapy. The specialist treatment of mental disturbance demands such extensive training, and such wide knowledge of the inter-relation of emotions with their physical expressions, their characterological defences and disguises, and their morbid manifestations, that it is of necessity a wholetime profession.

Yet, for all that, the psychotherapeutic specialist deals with the same problems, conflicts, and mental pains that are the very stuff of all human unhappiness and suffering. His experience must throw light on these matters which is important for all who are concerned to help their fellows. It seems useful, therefore, to set forth what is generally illuminating (as distinct from what is too involved in technical details) in the psychotherapist's expanding knowledge. Those we seek to help are a prey to *anxiety*, or, as I prefer here to call it, *mental pain*. We will therefore consider first the fact of mental pain, and then the defences most usually built up against it, and finally its external and internal causes and the possibilities of cure. We shall approach this task in a religio-scientific way, seeking to unite love and understanding in one approach.

Before we proceed, one further fact must be borne in mind. It has to be admitted that our willingness to accept the findings of science about the bodily, and about the mental, aspects of our human nature are not on the same footing. It is not that psychological theories may be wrong, or premature in formulation and open to revision. So may physiological and bacteriological theories be wrong. The history of medical science, like that of all other sciences is strewn with discarded hypotheses: so also is the history of psychoanalysis, and so also, surely, is the history of theology. Furthermore, the history of medicine is also marked by therapeutic fashions in the purely physical realm, even more obviously than in the psychiatric. In all these matters psychotherapy is not on any different footing from any other branch of medicine or science, and its theories must be subjected to constant critical examination and revision.

Our reluctance to accept the psychoanalytical *approach* itself, is primarily due to the fact that *human beings have a very strong interest in discovering the causes of their troubles anywhere rather than in their own mind.* Sometimes our troubles we insist are due to our neighbours, or workmates, or the government or social system or economic order: or, again, to some hostile foreign power which is undermining our position in the world and making life hard for us. But, if we are driven to recognize that all is not well within ourselves, then it must be in our body, not in our mind. It is almost impossible, apart from direct psychoanalytical experience, to realize how strong an interest human beings have in locating the seat of personal trouble in the body and not in the mind. Some idea of this will emerge presently when we come to consider defences against anxiety; in passing we may say that, in the course of psychoanalytical treatment, it is common to find a patient oscillating for a considerable time between insight into and awareness of a mental problem on the one hand, and the flaring up of a physical symptom on the other. *When the physical symptom returns, insight is lost and consciousness of the trouble in the mind disappears. When the physical disturbance is relinquished, then the real disturbance in the mind emerges once again.* Hence the term 'conversion hysteria', where a psychological tension is converted into a physiological disturbance. The tendency many people show to accept eagerly physical diagnosis and treatments, while they are hostile to psychotherapy, is bound up with their entire system of defences against mental pain.

One day I was in the room of a psychiatrist in the Leeds Department when the telephone bell rang. I answered the call and an irate voice said 'Is that Dr. So and So?' I said 'No, can I give him a message?' The man answered 'Yes, tell him to cancel my appointment. I don't want a psychiatrist. What on earth does my G.P. mean by it, arranging for me to see a psychiatrist? I shall tell him what I think of him. There's nothing wrong with me mentally. I've got a duodenal ulcer.' I answered gently, 'Well, you sound very tense. Duodenal ulcer goes with emotional tensions, so I think you'd be well advised to see Dr. So and So.' He slammed down the receiver without even remembering to give me his name. He preferred to keep his duodenal ulcer.

As soon as one starts looking into the real source of trouble, in the mental personality itself, people react with a rising tension of anxiety which, as we have seen, often finds expression in a hostile attack on psychology and all its works. Ministers of religion draw the same kind of hostile response in fact, but it is masked under traditional acceptance and politeness, and is less intense because the minister of religion does not threaten to lay bare the deeper levels of unconscious anxiety in people's minds. Ministers of religion generally aid people's defences against the dangers menacing them from their unconscious, either by giving comfort and support, or else by arousing guilt and so increasing the forces of repression. The significance of that statement will only become apparent later. The psychoanalyst arouses the deepest anxiety by leading patients behind their defences to the internal dangers by which they feel menaced.

Nevertheless, both parson and psychotherapist direct people's attention back upon themselves and arouse in the minds of those they seek to help an immediate 'resistance'. The fact, and amazing strength, of this resistance to treatment, which is automatic, emotional, and in origin unconscious, was one of the earliest and most important of all Freud's discoveries. The psychiatrist now shares with the parson the honour of being the popular butt of jokes, caricatures and cartoons, and even threatens to displace the parson in that rôle. It is an admission of his importance but also an expression of the uneasiness and hostility felt about what he has to say.

Human beings feel safer, calmer, and less anxious if they can find scapegoats for their troubles. They try if possible to find an *external scapegoat*—nazis, communists, capitalists, the government, the political party that is not one's own; or, coming nearer home, their employer, or annoying neighbour, or their minister who didn't visit them or doesn't fill the church or isn't like the last minister, or else even their husband, wife or children. If they are driven to the unwelcome discovery that something is wrong inside themselves, then they will definitely prefer to make their body the scapegoat. That is why it is much harder to accept scientific findings about the mind than about the body, at least in relation to ourselves. People are often very willing to take what they believe to be a psychological line about other people's illnesses and to use the term 'neurotic' illegitimately as a term of criticism or abuse, as if it meant 'conscious playing up'. But the critic's own physical symptoms of nervous tension must of course be taken as genuinely physically caused.

The psychotherapeutic approach directs our attention to what we most want to conceal, ignore and repress in ourselves, and that is why there can be no easy, light-hearted, slick approach to the problems of therapy for mental pain. This statement will most probably be interpreted, at this stage, in a moral sense, as if it meant that the psychotherapist is bent on trying to make people recognize their faults and bad impulses and socially unacceptable character traits. We must leave to a later chapter the explanation of the fact that this moral interpretation is not the correct one: the present purpose is rather to make clear that psychotherapy is inevitably an extremely difficult task which offers no genuine short cuts if radical results are to be achieved: for it involves exploring the innermost secret recesses of the personality where nothing can be touched without at least temporarily increasing the conscious mental pain of one who is already suffering.

CHAPTER II

Physical Pain and Anxiety

WE have seen that the first and most important thing about the troubled person who seeks ministerial or psychotherapeutic aid is that he is in pain, and that if he has pain in his body it is even more important to realize that that most likely masks pain in his mind. Human beings shrink from pain, and ultimately they shrink from mental pain even more than from bodily pain. In fact slight pains in the body may panic a person solely because they secretly represent intolerable mental pains. The ability to endure physical pain often depends on the degree of mental pain hidden behind it. It is not the actual amount of physical suffering endured at the dentist's, for example, that makes people so abnormally afraid of having their teeth attended to. It is the whole imaginative situation as presented to the mind, and even more the wholly unconscious significance read into dentistry, that account for the fears which are so out of proportion to the facts. Many patients under psychoanalysis produce dreams of going to the dentist irrespective of whether at the time they are undergoing any actual dental treatment, and these dreams show that the dentistry situation plays upon something very deep and fear-laden in their unconscious.

The natural human shrinking from pain often makes people suffering from some physical trouble go on enduring it rather than face the pain of treatment. There are other emotional factors involved in this as well, but one sees particularly clearly in the case of children and nervous adults how, for example, they will put up with the throbbing and nagging of a festered finger rather than endure having it lanced and the pus squeezed out. There is a strong tendency to endure, and get used to, and, if possible, ignore and forget whatever causes pain *while going on living with it*. This tendency, quite often observed in relation to physical pains, is a far more serious cause of stubborn refusal of, and resistance to, the treatment of mental pains. *It is as if human beings secretly hug to themselves and fear to lose whatever it is that acts as the fundamental cause of their mental pain.* We shall see presently that that is quite literally true.

This throws an additional important light on the resistance to, and evasion of, any attempt to help people to drop their defences against mental pain and become aware of the real trouble. It is part of the total problem, that they cannot help resisting and evading, and they do not consciously know why. It seems simple enough, if people evade the recognition of their real difficulties by seeking scapegoats in other people or in their body, to say 'Very well, let us make them face the facts and come to grips with themselves.' Before any such ruthless line is taken it is well to appreciate what facts it is they have to face, and whether, in fact, it is possible for them to face them by themselves. It is more than likely that some particular person who conspicuously and habitually blames everyone around him for his unhappiness and suffering, would be driven into a suicide compulsion or nervous breakdown if, without further help, he suddenly ceased to project his troubles in this way. For *projection is one of the great defences of human beings against internal dangers.* Often, under analysis, patients will shut down on dreams and their inner mental situation, and try to talk of nothing but their external difficulties.

We have referred to the fact that *physical ill-health may be another such defence.* Physical illness is not simply an evil to get rid of: it has a positive rôle to play. On this matter the utilitarian point of view, and also the moral point of view, may appear to clash with the psychotherapeutic viewpoint. The general medical attitude will be that the obvious thing to do with any physical illness is to get rid of it by appropriate treatment. The moral attitude would appear to be that if the physical symptoms mask mental problems which are the real trouble then it is not right to tolerate evasions, self deceptions and illusions. Yet looked at psychologically we may have to admit that a physical illness is a defensive barrier against the arousal of an anxiety-state severe enough to endanger mental stability, and the physical symptoms may be the lesser of two evils.

It is often unwise to rid an elderly person of a physical complaint if there be reason to suspect that it is psychogenic. It may turn out that the bodily disturbance is an escape from, and a protection against, a much more intolerable mental disturbance of the nature of, say, depression, or persecutory anxiety: and the elderly person no longer has the mental resilience needed to solve the psychic problem. That is why, often, people who are cured of one bodily ill are liable to develop another one in its place after a time. This is of great practical importance for the understanding of many difficult people. Every minister of religion comes across people who are hypochondriacal, always worrying over some imaginary complaint. If you succeed in reassuring them about one, they soon invent another. Their friends lose patience with them after a time; you may feel inclined to blame them as self-indulgent and self-pitying, and accuse them of only trying to draw sympathy. But clearly such people have a compelling need for a bodily complaint to attach their anxiety to. Since the bodily complaints of the hypochondriac are not real, they cannot be the source of the anxiety from which these people suffer. They have to invent a bodily scapegoat to lay their burden of anxiety upon, otherwise they will have to face the acute mental pain of conscious awareness of their real trouble. Before an attempt is made to drive people out of hypochondriacal defences, or to cure them of a genuine though psychogenic physical illness, it is necessary to know whether their real anxiety is of a kind which it is possible for them to face.

All this can be most easily made plain by means of actual examples. An older middle-aged man of splendid physique, and who was pronounced by his doctor to be organically sound, had tortured himself for several years by worrying successively over his heart, lungs, kidneys, liver, stomach and so on. He developed real pains in the areas he believed to be affected. As soon as his doctor disposed of one possibility, he would develop another, in each case feeling quite sure there was something seriously wrong and suffering genuine physical discomfort which, however, shifted from one organ to another. Finally he felt convinced that there was something seriously wrong somewhere which the doctor had not discovered. He was, of course, quite right. No one *can* get into such a condition without there being a real and adequate cause, but it was not in his body. It was in his mind, and so long as his hypochondriacal condition was kept going he was spared the consciousness of mental pain.

As he talked to me it emerged that just before this hydra-headed illness began, his son had been killed in the war. He did not think there was any connection between the two things, but he went on to describe how he had braced himself to show no grief for his wife's sake. He must not break down whatever happened and all his friends marvelled how well he took the blow. But soon afterwards he began to develop these nagging anxieties about bodily illness. He felt quite *depressed* about his health. His wife felt *depressed* about the death of their son and openly expressed and cried out her grief and remained bodily well. The father told me he had just dreamed that this son came home on leave and he had cycled part way back to his camp with him and they enjoyed a good *tête-à-tête* on the way. I simply remarked: 'Wouldn't it be fine if you could really do that now? But he's dead and you can't.' The man burst into tears and sobbed for the first time, for nearly an hour, for two consecutive sessions, developing a splitting headache, and breaking out into sobbing at home on the slightest provocation. The next session after that he talked calmly but with real feeling about the boy and his own grief; and his bodily pains and worries disappeared.

The psychotherapist feels he is in luck's way with a case as simple as that. Usually the anxieties concealed by hypochondria have a less important real precipitant in the present day, and their ultimate causes are deeply buried in the mind, of long standing, with origins in early life, and are part of the very structure of the personality. They cannot be easily or quickly eliminated. The important point is that *so often physical pain covers over mental pain and is a valuable defence against it.*

If that is true of hypochondriasis and of hysteria, it is also true of genuine bodily illness. Not all organic disease is psychogenic, but more and more diseases are now coming into the class of psychosomatic disorders, where organic illness is linked to mental and nervous tensions. On the one hand are the hysteric aches and pains, backaches, neuritis in limbs, headaches and even paralyses; on the other hand there are the general anxiety-symptoms such as palpitation, perspiration, indigestion, tremor, leading steadily on to the far more serious psychosomatic group of diseases such as gastric and duodenal ulcer, sinusitis, glandular disturbances, asthma, eczemas, heart affections such as thrombosis and so on. Behind all these ailments of the body there lies mental pain, and serious disturbances of the personality. Furthermore, organic illness which is not psychogenic may still give a much needed respite from mental pain.

These facts may be illustrated by two cases of eczema. An elderly lady developed a chronic running eczema, which spread at times all over her body, not long after her husband died. All the resources of medical treatment for over a year produced no more than improvements which were always followed by relapse again. Finally, this woman was cured by a motherly and sympathetic woman herbalist who personally massaged a wonderful ointment into the affected areas, spending a long time with her, and talking soothingly to her meanwhile. The eczema masked a severe depression brought on by her husband's death. The purely physical medical treatments failed to cure her eczema because the doctors had nothing to give her in its place as a better defence against her mental pain. The herbalist cured her, not by means of the wonderful ointment which could not have contained any ingredients unknown to the doctors, but by the motherly personal relationship, and the soothing and caressingly intimate bodily attention, and the sympathetic interest not confined to a hurried professional visit, diagnosis and prescription, but extended over considerable periods of time spent on and with the patient. Here was something better than eczema to keep depression at bay. Here was something capable of relieving the intense and frightening sense of loneliness, and the proof that the world was still a safe and friendly place in which kindly personal relationships existed. Here was an opportunity to talk out to an 'accepting' listener the pains of grief, the guilty regrets over whether one had done all one ought to have done for the lost loved one in his life time, the anxious looking ahead and fears of solitude, and so on. The eczema could not be given up if it merely meant encountering the full blast of a crippling depression without help for that.

A patient of mine under psychoanalytical treatment was suddenly faced with the possibility of her parents removal to another town. Rapidly an intensely irritating eczema broke out on both hands. She made matters worse by clawing and scratching at one hand with the other till they were raw and bleeding. In talking of this 'clawing and scratching' the patient drifted quickly on to her feelings of anger and resentment at having her home snatched away and being forced to live in digs. This anger she was venting on herself in attacking the hands that irritated her, thereby becoming less aware of her painful resentment against her parents. This bit of 'talking out' led to a slight initial improvement, and then suddenly the parents decided not to remove, and the whole eczema cleared up. It was plainly a defence against acute developing separation-anxiety in a very dependent person.

When we are simply aiming to illustrate and establish a basic fact, it is unnecessary—and space forbids—to cite cases of all the other psychosomatic and hysteric illnesses. The optimistic ideal of the progress of physical medicine and the discovery of more and more wonderful drugs, till all physical illness is mastered, is something of a phantasy. The fact is that the more progress physical medicine has made, the more psychological illness has been unmasked and forced to the front. Physical illness, for many people, cannot be dispensed with until we have found out how to rid the human mind of its stores of unconscious repressed anxiety. Where that mental pain is so severe that the sufferer cannot cope with it if it is drawn into consciousness, then it will be repressed and turned into bodily pain which is easier to bear than mental pain: or else it will be dammed up behind one or more of the other defences which we shall presently examine. Often, therefore, it is not simply a question of getting rid of bodily illness *per se*, but of whether you can give the patient something better to put in its place, either as a defence against, or more radically to bring about a reduction of, mental pain.

There are many people who have been so hardly dealt with in life from the start, their personalities are so deeply disturbed emotionally, and their minds at deep unconscious levels are so occupied by bitter conflict-situations in which unsatisfied need, fear, hate and guilt are constantly aroused that they have no chance at all of ever being fully healthy, happy, creative and well-adjusted. So far as we can tell at present it may be possible for a human being to be so grossly disturbed in mental development in early life that abnormalities are set up which cannot be reversed or cured in later life. The results of neglect, illness or accident on the body in very early life often quite visibly become permanent and unalterable. Tissues take on forms which, however disadvantageous, do not admit of further change. It seems possible, when we consider psychotic, psychopathic and grossly neurotic personalities, that something analogous to these irreversible abnormalities can happen in *mental* development. The structural organization, and therefore the emotional and impulsive functioning, of the mind can become so set in fixed patterns at an early age, that it seems impossible to modify them in extreme cases. The personality apparently becomes impervious to any mellowing or healing influence. Good examples of such types in literature are Heathcliffe in *Wuthering Heights,* or Dicken's *Fagin,* and in real life, the sadistic inhuman beings who carried out concentration camp tortures. In the sphere of psychotic illness, mental hospitals provide both shelter for the too grossly abnormal, and protection for society. But we cannot be content with such a pessimistic conclusion. At least psychoanalysis is now in a position to say that *one of the major factors barring the way to profound changes of personality is that the breaking up of the rigidities of personality based on repression and other mental defences can expose a person to so much mental pain that he cannot or will not stand it alone*: and every therapeutic effort to reach the core of his problem is blocked by stubborn resistances, which only yield slowly in proportion as he comes to feel more and more safe with his analyst.

Re-creative love allied to scientific understanding may be able to achieve more than we yet know. How can we help people to stand up to severe mental pain with sufficient success to enable them to undergo a regrowth of their personality structure? Anything short of that can only be a supportive therapy which bolsters up the ego, and strengthens its defences against internal dangers which are not in themselves removed. If, however, we are to understand how mental pain can be alleviated we must also understand how it is caused, and what are the natural spontaneous defences against it that all human minds automatically set up. We shall find that this enquiry will take us deeper into the realms of both psychiatric and religious experience.

As to the forms of mental pain, common sense understanding takes us little further than the fixing of labels on familiar states of mental distress. We are all roughly familiar with such unpleasant feelings as worry, anxiety, apprehension, fear, guilt, sorrow, grief, and depression. Large numbers of people experience these mental distresses to an extent which finds no adequate cause in contemporary external circumstances. Evidently these forms of mental pain can have hidden internal causes which are part of the very mental 'make-up' of the individuals in question. Unhappy or disturbing outer events play upon something which is not apparent, i.e. is unconscious, in the mind.

But there are more severe forms of these above mentioned mental pains: fear can become terror, guilt can become intolerable dread of punishment and the morbid fear of having committed the unforgivable sin, anxiety and apprehension can become utterly paralysing, grief and depression can become crippling melancholia; just as anger can become destructive rage. In barbarous times when the social order provided no very high degree of security, it was a commonplace thing to experience these emotional states in extreme forms in the face of external dangers. Civilization normally protects us against the worst insecurities and spares us the more intolerable forms of mental pain in our ordinary daily life. But there are two exceptions; war and infancy. We have known in wartime the more violent and disintegrating forms of mental pain. It is, however, little realized by people in general that *the infant is a prey to emotional disturbances of the most violent order*. The infant mind is as yet so little organized, and has hardly begun to develop any apparatus of emotional self-control. Feeling and impulse are aroused rapidly and run riot in the mind. Within a short time a baby's crying can work up into a blinding, stifling, convulsive, volcanic eruption of its whole being which certainly terrifies the infant. We shall see that we have to go back to these things to understand the origins and deepest causes of mental pain. Infantile experience is not just happily grown out of and left behind. It forms the starting point of all mental development and is built into the personality as its unconscious foundation. It is psychoanalysis which, for the first time in human history, has revealed to us the fact that *a very large part of our adult character, beliefs, interests and activities, in addition to their objective significance, constitutes a well-knit defensive barrier against the outbreak in consciousness of intense anxieties of very early origin which persist in the unconscious areas of our mental life.* Before going into the question of the ultimate nature of the hidden cause of mental pain, it is necessary to look further into these defences.

Meanwhile we close this chapter with an illuminating reference to Kipling as presented by Professor Bonamy Dobree in a Third Programme broadcast talk. 'He spoke of the poet's interest in mental breakdown and his knowledge of inner mental hells and horrors which have "to be experienced to be appreciated". "In his younger days he was eager only to tell the stories as part of the enthralling, darkly striated, pageant of life; later he became interested in the causes, and finally he was absorbed in the healing of the horror." Dobree refers to the charge that Kipling was "callous about physical pain" but replies that he knew it was as nothing compared with spiritual agony. This he states unequivocally in the *Hymn to Physical Pain*:

> Dread Mother of Forgetfulness
>   Who, when Thy reign begins,
> Wipest away the Soul's distress
>   And memory of her sins. . . .
>
> Wherefore we praise Thee in the deep,
>   And on our beds we pray
> For Thy return, that Thou may'st keep
>   The Pains of Hell at bay.
>
>   (*The Listener*, 12th June, 1952, p. 967.)

That is the situation the psychotherapist faces.' (H. Guntrip, 'The Therapeutic Factor in Psychotherapy', *British Journal of Medical Psychology*, 1953, vol. xxvi, Pt. 2, p. 120.)

CHAPTER III

The Nature and Origin of Anxiety: Needs and Fears

I. ANXIETY

IT is usually said that anxiety is the cause of neurosis, behaviour disorders and character malformations. But anxiety must be *about* something. Anxiety, or, as I have here called it 'mental pain', is certainly a cause of further ill effects, but is itself an effect of, and a response to, some deeper primary cause. What is anxiety? Is there more than one kind of anxiety? How does anxiety find an apparently permanent and actively persisting place in the very foundations of our personality? These are the questions with which we must begin the more detailed study of mental pain. 'Why are ye fearful O ye of little faith?' (Matt. viii, v. 26), and since it is so clearly the common lot of all human beings to be 'fearful', the question is less of a rebuke than a challenge to find a really adequate answer. Why indeed are human beings of every type, class and race so chronically fear-ridden, so that it is somewhat rare to meet the person who impresses as being genuinely calm and non-anxious, balanced and stable, and deeply at peace within himself whatever he faces in his outer life?

Most of us are in varying degrees somewhat tense, and prone to the irritability that betrays an anxious and insecure mind, whenever our environment is less than thoroughly supporting. Yet this omnipresent anxiety is not just a simple reaction to real difficulties and dangers in our outer world. It is well known to us that 'worrying' and an apprehensive attitude to life can be a characteristic of a person irrespective of whether his or her actual material existence gives cause for worry or not. Anxiety is so often the characteristic atmosphere of the inner mental life, as if we developed and produced anxiety continuously from some hidden inner region in our personality without knowing how, and without being able to stop doing it.

We will first turn for help in answering our questions to two psychoanalysts who have made notable contributions: Dr. Phyllis Greenacre (Professor of Clinical Psychiatry, Cornell University Medical College, New York) and Mrs. Melanie Klein (the pioneer children's analyst). Professor Greenacre deals with certain facts of which we ought at least to be aware, and she takes us back to the very beginnings of human life in birth and the ante-natal period. We need only summarize briefly, as a starting point for our enquiry, the views she puts forward in *Trauma, Growth and Personality* (Hogarth Press, 1953). Her general theme is that 'Trauma' (i.e. any fact, situation or event whether physical or mental that has an *injurious* effect on the infant and growing child), leads, in the processes of growth, to a persisting condition of 'anxiety-proneness', and to the storing up of anxiety-producing factors in the very structure of the developing personality.

Professor Greenacre distinguishes between *Basic Anxiety* and *Neurotic Anxiety*, and it is particularly to her theory of *Basic Anxiety* that I wish to refer. She regards Basic Anxiety as having no very definite psychological content, but as being largely organic in nature, while Neurotic Anxiety has very definite psychological content. Basic Anxiety originates as a result of traumatic factors impinging on the infant in the ante-natal period, in the birth-process, and in the immediate post-natal months. Neurotic Anxiety originates as a result of the child's further development under the influence of disturbing, traumatic, personal relationships in the family life which is the medium in which the foundations of the child's psychic personality structure are grown. She advances:

'the tentative hypothesis that severe suffering and frustration occurring in the ante-natal and early post-natal months, especially in the period preceding speech development, leave a heightened organic stamp on the make-up of the child. This is so assimilated into his organization as to be almost if not entirely indistinguishable from the inherited constitutional factors which themselves can never be entirely isolated and must rather be assumed from the difficult maze of observations of the genetic background of the given individual. I believe this organic stamp of suffering to consist of a genuine physiological sensitivity, a kind of increased indelibility of reaction to experience which heightens the anxiety potential and gives greater resonance to the anxieties of later life' (p. 50). 'Painful or uncomfortable situations of the earliest post-natal weeks, before the psychological content or the means of defence have been greatly elaborated, would ... tend to increase the organic components of the anxiety reaction' (p. 49).

Here is a fundamental thing. Emotional and other disturbances of the mother during pregnancy, a difficult birth and unwise or unskilful handling in the first few months of separate life, misfortunes that in some degree must befall most human beings, start the baby off with *an increased organic and quantitative liability to experience anxiety-tensions readily, along with a decreased internal capacity to tolerate and master such tensions.*

This Basic Anxiety is not a constitutional factor but Greenacre believes that it occurs so early that it fuses with constitutional factors. It would seem that fortunate and happy later childhood experience can reduce it, and can consolidate adequate mental defences to contain and master it. On the other hand it is the basis of quantitatively increased anxiety reactions to all later difficulties, thus intensifying those anxieties of the developmental period which have specific psychological content, and which set up the neurotic element in the personality.

Greenacre clearly distinguishes the *Essential Neurosis* from this Basic *Anxiety*. Anxieties originating in the disturbed or neurotic area of the personality have psychological content and are open to psychoanalytical investigation. For the clarification of these anxieties we turn to Melanie Klein who has made a most important contribution to the problem with her distinction between *persecutory* and *depressive* anxiety. We become anxious both when we ourselves are endangered by external or internal[1] persecutors, hostile, aggressive figures who menace us with injury and possibly destruction: and also when these dangers threaten our love-objects to whom we are bound by all our deepest needs. Persecutory anxiety is fear for ourselves, depressive anxiety is fear for those we need and love. These are the anxieties that develop in the period when the infant is in process of becoming a distinct individual experiencing highly significant relationships with the other persons in the family.

Thus it would seem to represent the situation accurately if we say that in the first case the need for *self-preservation* is involved, and in the second the need for *the preservation of good-object relationships*. In this case the two basic fears would be the *fear of death* and the *fear of object-loss*. But it is difficult to keep these distinct. For the baby, object-loss, which in its most fundamental form is loss of mother, would involve death (at least by neglect if not by attack and destruction) while death involves object-loss and loss of all those satisfactions that make it worthwhile to cling to life. The fears of *destruction* and of *frustration* or *deprivation* along with their underlying needs, are fundamentally related.

Freud did not believe that a fear of death existed in the unconscious. Melanie Klein believes that the fear of death is fundamental in the unconscious as well as the conscious. But the concept of a fear of death calls for careful study. Death is often regarded as affording a welcome release from suffering. The need for self-preservation implies a desire to go on existing, but one must evidently have a motive for going on existing. We not seldom find patients in whom this desire has dwindled to very insignificant proportions. They have lost interest in everything, life seems futile and they wish to die. We find always that such patients have lost the will-to-live because they have lost the capacity to effect anything like

[1] Internal persecutors. See p. 44.

genuine *rapport* and relationship with the outer world. They are aloof, cut off, schizoid. Their suicidal wishes are different from the angry suicidal impulse springing from inturned hate in the depressed person. It is a case of the collapse of object-seeking libido;[1] not of the upsurge of object-destroying aggression. One such patient said 'I'd be better dead, I'm of no use to anyone. My family would be better off without me. My feelings are dead. I feel nothing for anyone and life has no meaning.' When personal object-relations break down completely, when the very desire for good-object relations is so starved and hungry and greedy that one's need itself seems to have become destructive and is therefore stifled, then the need for self-preservation dies as well. One patient remarked, 'I'm afraid I couldn't make moderate demands on anyone, so I don't make any demands at all', and complained that life seemed pointless, one might as well be dead.

We must conclude that *the desire for self-preservation is a desire, not for the prolongation of bare existence as such, but of a significant existence, a desire for a continuance of the opportunity for self-realization in, and by means of, good relationships with other persons*. In the absence of the possibility of a meaningful life, death may appear as a welcome relief. What is feared then, is not death *per se*, but on the one hand the loss of living satisfactions in good personal relations, and on the other the terror of being subjected to a cruel and mutilating attack, of living and being tortured and persecuted, of suffering a persisting 'living death' in a continuing bad-object relationship. That this is the situation experienced in the unconscious as the source of the most acute persecutory anxiety is evident from the fact of the frequent occurrence of nightmares in many people, recurring dreams of being tortured in a concentration camp from which they cannot escape, or from one

---

[1] 'Libido' is the psychoanalytical term for the basic life-urge, the desire and drive to live, to love, to achieve good relations with the object world. Freud regarded it more narrowly as the sexual drive, though he broadened the definition of sexual. Fairbairn regards the sexual drive as only a part of libido.

patient's dream of being locked in a prison cell, bound with ropes, and being continually run through the body by the gaoler with his rapier. The fear of death arises spontaneously when self-destructive forces operate internally in the personality to crush and inhibit the life-forces, the libidinal striving towards good-object relationships.

Our fundamental need, the need that defines and characterizes our nature as human beings, is the need to relate ourselves libidinally, not aggressively, and significantly to other human beings and so to grow up and live as persons, not as biological automata. *Anxiety is our reaction in face of any threat of destruction of the possibility of good-object relationships,* either by the destruction of ourselves or of our love-objects and the experiencing of the loss of good-objects coupled with being left at the mercy of inescapable bondage to persecuting bad-objects. We must conclude that what Karen Horney calls 'basic anxiety'[1] arises out of frustration of 'basic need', and that *the primary phenomenon in human beings is 'the tension of basic need' which is to be recognized as 'object-need'*, the need for some person or persons to whom we can relate ourselves significantly so that life can be positively enjoyed, and come to have a meaning and value, and to be worth preserving. This need begins as the baby's need for the breast and develops into the mature person's need for full personal relationships.

Fear arises with any threat or danger to the satisfaction of this object-need, either through losing good-objects or only having bad-objects. Yet so powerful is this object-need that if the child despairs of acquiring good-objects and is shut up in the power of bad-objects he will prefer mentally and materially to cling to his bad-objects rather than have none. But he is then doomed to live in a state of persisting anxiety and may be even terror, and he will set up and repress within himself a mental replica of the bad situation in its entirety. Fear is then generalized into persisting neurotic anxiety by the endopsychic

[1] Horney's 'Basic Anxiety' is not the same as Greenacre's. It is the fundamental neurotic anxiety arising specifically out of human relationships in childhood.

structural persistence of such bad-object situations. They constitute an abiding unhappy inner world in which the child grows up to live in perpetual fear and may be even extreme terror: for, once repressed and kept out of touch with corrective contact with the outer, materially real world, the psychic and phantasied bad objects in the unconscious[1] become steadily exaggerated as a result of the mounting tension of dammed up emotion, till they reach a pitch of frightfulness expressed in the images of persecuting and torturing wild animals, witches, ghosts and devils, and appear as such in nightmares. Myth, folk-lore and fairy tale, and the dreams of present day people abound in such bad figures which have a tenacious hold on their mental existence.

Fairbairn has pointed out that *tension* is the *tension of object-seeking needs*, the tension of needs for good-object relationships. In connection with this *primary tension of love-needs* there arise the *secondary tensions of hate*, i.e. of basic anxiety or neurotic fear and of basic hostility or neurotic aggression experienced in bad-object relationships.

This brief and somewhat formal schematic representation of the primary nature and *origin of anxiety or mental pain, as accompanying the tensions of unsatisfied need, unrelieved fear and undischarged aggression*, does little to bring home to us the disturbing intensity of the experience of it. Broadly speaking it is still generally assumed that the causes of anxiety, i.e. of deprivation, fear and resentment, are always to be looked for in our outer world, so that if a given person has no objective cause for anxiety in his environment and circumstances of the present day, it is supposed that he ought to be quite free from worry and should be happy and contented. It is part and parcel of this unrealistic view, that it is still almost universally and automatically assumed that the obvious cure for anxiety-states and nervous illness is an environmental change for the better. The anxious person himself often makes the same assumption. The cry of the person worn down by nagging anxiety is so often 'If only I could get away from my present life, I'd be

[1] Cp. p. 41.

better'. 'If only I could have a holiday or more leisure, live in a different neighbourhood, or have a better house, job, neighbours, husband or wife, all would be well.' The fact that real causes for anxiety can exist in the mental make-up itself is not clearly grasped even when it is suspected.

There is often naturally some justice in these complaints. Difficult circumstances, however, play upon internal causes of anxiety, and usually difficult circumstances would be much more successfully managed if there were no problems inside the personality itself.

It is by no means generally understood that *all human beings live in two worlds at the same time, an outer material world and an inner mental world* and that these two worlds do not coincide. Most people are today *verbally* familiar with the idea of the unconscious mind but they have little feeling for its reality, for the simple reason that it is unconscious. It plays no obvious and open part in our everyday life, until one learns to recognize the signs of its presence and power. The general assumption in practice is still that our 'mind' is simply our *conscious* ways of perceiving, feeling and thinking about our outer world.

The idea that our mind is not only a means of reacting to the outer world, but also that it is itself a second, inner world of psychic realities is not generally understood. It constitutes at one and the same time the nature of our self, our personal mental make up, by virtue of which we react to outer objects and situations, and also a subjective world distinct from the outer world. We live also in this subjective world where we have to deal with objects and situations which only have a mental existence but nevertheless constantly arouse in us emotions and impulses every bit as real and urgent as those aroused by outer reality. We catch a glimpse of how real our inner mental world is when we give it hallucinatory form in dreams. This inner world is largely unconscious and perpetuates the world of our infancy and childhood, not so much in its happy aspects (that usually remains with us as consciously accessible memory), as in its *unhappy aspects as we experienced*

*them with all the limitations and distortions of the undeveloped
and inexperienced infant's point of view.*

This disturbing inner world occasionally becomes conscious
to us in the form of active phantasies, i.e. dreams and day-
dreams. It is, however, not simply a world of phantasies but
the unconscious area of our personality or self in a structural
sense. Our phantasies in their entirety express our mental
make-up. We have to understand that this internal mental
reality is at one and the same time *our self*, i.e. it is in its
entirety inside our total psyche, and also *a world of mental
objects and situations in which we live* and, for the most part,
suffer inside ourselves. This fact of *living inside a mental world
which is itself inside us* is clearly illustrated in dreams. A typical
dream is first a place, fields, buildings, a house or room, a
locality which, though often 'imaginatively invented' is also
frequently an actual place associated with our past life. Many
a dream begins 'I was a child again and back in the old school'
or 'back in the house where I was born'. Into this scene from
early life the dream then introduces living beings, animals,
persons or sometimes bizarre and wholly symbolic figures
such as sinister men, burglars, witches, devils, ghosts. These
'persons' inhabiting our 'dream localities' both include, and,
as symbols, reduce to, the significant people among whom we
passed our childhood, and above all the mother and father.
Thus in dreams adult people continue to meet and have
dealings with their parents often years after those parents have
died.

Finally, into the dream enters the dreamer himself, either
in his own person or disguised in some symbolic fashion.
Often the dreamer enters his dream only as a spectator of the
action that is going on, showing how much he seeks to keep
himself dissociated from his own inner world. But when he
enters into his own dream world as a principal actor on the
stage of inner psychic reality, then he is liable to wake and
find himself actually in the grip of the emotions aroused within, and the dream may have reached nightmare intensity.

All this busy inner life out of which our basic emotions

arise is hidden away during our waking hours behind an iron curtain of repression, while the outer world engages all our conscious attention. Yet we are not without clues as to its existence if we are prepared to recognize them. One person will say 'I'm always worried and yet I've got nothing really to worry about'. Perhaps not in outer reality, but it will be found that there is plenty to worry about in the unconscious inner world if and when it can be brought to view. Another person will explode emotionally with far more feeling than is called for by trivial events. The excess of feeling is drawn out of this inner world, the trivial event has touched on something that is going on in inner reality and brought about a sudden uprush of reaction. Yet a third stable person always feels slightly depressed for no obvious reason. The reason is within. Dreams and day dreams are eruptions of the inner world; so are neurotic symptoms, moods and irrational behaviour disorders. Much of the conscious personality and character is built as a defence against, and a means of control over, this inner world.

In this hidden region lie the ultimate causes of neurotic suffering, and of that mental pain which, whether it emerges as conscious anxiety or is masked by physical pain, forms the persisting undertone of mental life. In this inner world, *at its worst*, parts of the self suffer the pains of hell, tormented by persecuting devils, as nightmares all too often reveal.

We have seen that human beings are liable to suffer from three different kinds of tension dammed up within the psyche and the bodily organism to create troubles of both behaviour and health: (1) the tension of unsatisfied need, (2) the tension of fear, and (3) the tension of anger. Unsatisfied need arises out of object-loss, but this does not necessarily mean the sheer disappearance of the good object by death or desertion. It more usually means being confronted by an exciting, greatly needed, desirable person who tantalizingly withholds satisfaction and fails to give a relationship: such as a rather cold, practical mother to whom the child looks in vain for warm-hearted affection. This tantalizing figure, which Fairbairn calls the 'Exciting Object', and which I have called 'the Desirable Deserter' (*British Journal of Med. Psych.*, Vol. XXV, Pts. 2 and 3, 1952, p. 90) is constantly met with in the dreams and phantasies of patients, always arousing never-satisfied desires, and keeping going an unremitting state of pressing neediness and libidinal tension, accompanied by frustration-anger and aggression.

The tension of fear is also kept going in the unconscious world within by the presence of bad-objects, not only of the exciting and withholding type, but of the actively aggressive and persecuting type, called by Fairbairn the 'Rejecting Object', though this does not bring out their actively, aggressively angry and sadistic character. I have called this bad-object the 'Hated Denier' (op. cit. p. 90) but an essential characteristic is also that of 'destructive attacker'. This bad-object is a dangerous persecutor pure and simple, and in the unconscious the infantile ego lives in terror of it, and the whole psyche is permeated by fear. Need, anger and fear fuse into one complex tension and sustain persistent anxiety.

The persistence of these *fundamental tensions, of unsatisfied need, of anger and of fear*, can, of course, only be really relieved by the elimination of the internal bad-objects that arouse them. In view of the fact that these bad-objects are structural parts of the unconscious psyche, and that parts of the ego are tied to them in an equally structurally unconscious condition, it is clear that this involves a long process of considerable change and re-development, the process known as 'maturing' of the personality.

In the absence, however, of this radical 'cure' of maturing, the individual is bound to resort to whatever measures he can to relieve these painful tensions. Thus two different groups of tension-relieving processes are developed to ease the pressure, respectively, of needs or libidinal-tensions on the one hand and of anger-tensions and fear-tensions on the other. The first will take the form of *substitute gratifications* in the absence of good object-relationships. Compulsive masturbation or eating are examples. The second will take the form of *devices for discharging and reducing anger, fear and mental pain* to some more manageable and less disintegrating form than the primitive terror which is felt at the deepest unconscious levels. Conversion into physical symptoms is a case in point. Dreaming is a tension-relieving process that serves both groups. All these operations, which we shall presently study in some detail, partake of the nature of defences against, and attempts to minimize, the mental pain felt in this unconscious mental replica of early bad experiences.

It is pertinent to comment that, whereas in the early days of psychoanalysis sex was singled out as the great trouble-maker in human life, the emphasis has now for some time been shifting steadily on to anger and aggression, largely as a result of the work of Melanie Klein. Sexuality, in the narrower sense, comes more and more to be seen not as an isolated, disturbing, powerful instinct, but as a part of a larger whole. Sexuality is but one among other pathways along which flows our primary life-force, our basic active libidinal *need* for real good-object relationships in our outer life. In such relationships essential satisfaction and fulfilment can be found in the twin forms of emotional security and personal significance. One of the most striking things about deep psychoanalysis is the way it brings out the fact that at bottom patients do not know what a real personal relationship is. It comes to light that they had little experience of personal relationship as children in the home, and they have not got the 'feel' of its reality. They have never seen from the outside, or played a part in, the simple reality of two people understanding each other, respecting each other, feeling no rivalry towards each other but feeling straightforward affection for each other, finding pleasure in giving and receiving mutually, and having a stable trust in each other. Only in the setting of such a relationship can the more intense and passionate sexual desire for complete physical intimacy arise without anxieties.

In the setting of genuine satisfying personal relationship, the sexual urge does not become an unruly, compulsive craving. It is a bodily function which is spiritualized into a sacrament of mutual giving and taking, expressing the unity of two lives. In the absence of genuine personal relationship, the sexual urge is a biological drive, which is exploited in the interests of starved, hungry, angry, frustrated needs, and so it becomes possessive, demanding, compulsive and dangerous. The trouble lies not with sexuality, but with the anger and frustration felt at the lack of good-object relationships. One patient says: 'In my home the way people got on together was by constant nagging and criticism, taking each other up on every point, sharp shooting. We never had normal friendly conversations. If spoken to we all replied in a sharp tense way that got the other person's back up, and turned every conversation into an antagonistic argument.'

The frustration of libidinal needs for living in good personal relationships calls up reactions of rage, hate and fear. Thereafter 'need' becomes 'angry need' and 'frightened need'. The greater the anger and the more intense the aggressive destructive drive, the greater the fear. It is the ramifications of anger and aggression in the personality that are at the bottom of all the self-destructive mental and physical developments in neurosis. *The dammed up tensions resulting from the inevitable co-existence of starved needs and frustration-aggression give rise to the persisting anxiety-state we have designated as 'mental pain'.*

CHAPTER IV

A Digression into Psychoanalytical History

THE position outlined in Chapter III, as was indicated at the end of the chapter, contains much that is not representative of the orthodox classic theory of psychoanalysis as developed by Freud. It derives rather from neo-Freudian and post-Freudian developments and it will be useful briefly to indicate how these newer views are related to the older ones.

I use the term psychoanalytical psychology to cover not simply the classic Freudian school which laid the foundations, but all schools which make a fundamentally dynamic and analytical approach to the understanding of the impulsive and emotional side of human nature. This is in accordance with growing usage, despite the efforts of the strict Freudian school to reserve to themselves the monopoly of the term.

Thus Professor C. A. Mace, the Editor of the Pelican Psychology Series, writes in his editorial note: 'The term "psychoanalysis" is currently used to cover all those facts and theories presented in the words of Freud, Jung, and Adler, together with those of their associates, disciples, and intellectual heirs. It is so used despite persistent recommendations that it should be applied only to the theory and practice of Freud and his disciples. . . . It will no doubt continue to be so used until someone suggests a new convenient title for the genus as distinct from the species.' (In *An Introductoon to Jung's Psychology.* F. Fordham, p. 7.)

Psychoanalytical psychology contrasts with *academic psychology* which is mainly descriptive of the innate and developed abilities and capacities of individuals, and of their visible and fairly fixed personality-traits, as manifested, and open to scientific testing, in their conscious personality. One of the most important uses of this type of psychology is in vocational guidance, where it helps to fit the reasonably normal and stable person into his appropriate social function and his economic niche. *General psychiatry*, on the other hand, is mainly concerned with the medical problem of healing, which in practice means relieving symptoms by any methods found to be useful. Such methods will range all the way from the use of surgery, electricity, drugs, hospitalization, occupational and social therapy, to short-term individual psychotherapy. Such a wide range of treatments has to be considered for many cases that may not be suitable for deep psychoanalysis.

It is, however, *psychoanalytical psychology* in all its various shades that *studies the basic motivational dynamics of the human being as a whole person*, the growth and structure of his personality, his needs, wants, aims, the frustrations and unhappiness he meets, the breakdowns he experiences and the stability he may achieve. All forms of this approach owe their primary inspiration and quite a lot of their fundamental theory to the discoveries of Sigmund Freud.

Professor Mace, in the Editorial note above quoted, writes: ' "Psychoanalysis" in this broader sense covers both a set of theories and a set of practices. The most distinctive doctrine common to all the theories . . . is that the mind, psyche, or personality of man comprises unconscious as well as conscious components, and that man's behaviour and his conscious states can be explained only by reference to the unconscious sources of motivation. . . . The practice of psychoanalysis has grown out of, but is not restricted to, the treatment of mental illness, and it is probably common ground to all the schools that the success of the treatment depends in the last resort upon the patient's own (assisted) self-diagnosis and his own (assisted) self-rehabilitation.' (op. cit. pp. 7–8.)

That is a fair minimum statement made by a psychologist who is not a psychoanalyst but an interested and sympathetic observer.

In such a fundamental field of study it was unlikely that any one line of thought would hold a complete monopoly, nor would it have been healthy had it done so. Yet we are bound to admit that Freud's work has proved to be the indispensable and irreplaceable foundation on which all other workers, Jung, Adler, Horney, Fromm, Sullivan, and now Melanie Klein and Fairbairn, have built. Of all these later theoretical innovators, Klein and Fairbairn have kept closest to the strict and radical Freudian method of psychoanalytical investigation, and also to *Freud's all-important concept of a deep unconscious in which the life of childhood is in some sense preserved and perpetuated.*

Their work, however, developing from certain aspects of Freud's own theories, leads to a radically new conception of the nature and structure of this unconscious part of the human psyche. This, apparently, has not been recognized by Melanie Klein and her followers, but has been made explicit by Fairbairn.

Freudian theory came ultimately to rest on two distinct and different concepts, those of 'instinct' and of the 'super-ego'. *Instinct* is a primarily *biological* concept and denotes whatever are taken to be the innate, inherited, motivational factors. The *super-ego* is a purely psychological concept, that of the creation, as a result of developmental experience, of a controlling factor within the psyche which consists of a mental replica of parents, as the child experiences them in their disciplinary capacity. Klein retains the Freudian concept of instinct and develops the concept of the super-ego into that of a multiplicity of 'internal psychic objects' which 'internalize', or reproduce in mental form, many aspects, both bodily and mental, of parents and others who enter into the child's earliest life.

Fairbairn discards the concept of instinct, and utilizes the concept of internal objects as a means of elaborating a more purely psychological, and therefore 'personal', theory of the developing structure of human personality, particularly in its unconscious areas.

Freud established beyond reasonable doubt that *our familiar, conscious, socially oriented and adjusted self is only a part of our total self or psyche.* Nervous illness is due to the fact that there are other aspects of our mental life of which we are not conscious, excluded from ordinary access to our waking thoughts by active internal psychic repression. No one can make any direct statement about his own unconscious because it is unconscious and therefore not open to direct inspection. We all keep this area of our inner personal life cut off from immediate awareness and we stubbornly resist all attempts to bring it into consciousness, lest anxiety attacks should break out in us. We have thus an interest in denying its existence. The unconscious can only be known by special and indirect methods of investigation. Its reality and activity are betrayed by its effects when we can allow ourselves to recognize them.

Nevertheless, it can be so known. This hidden region of our mental life or these aspects of our personality about which we maintain a stubborn unawareness, can and do invade consciousness or influence consciousness in various disguised forms such as dreams, phantasies, emotional eruptions, compulsive irrational acts, and the symptoms of nervous illness. What is happening in the unconscious can also be inferred from the nature of the psychic defences we erect against it, among the most important of which are rigid character-traits designed to suppress impulses and attitudes of the opposite kind.

The unconscious area of the psyche is the disturber of our conscious peace, and according to Freud it consists of uncivilized and childish *impulses* which we still feel and against which we build up defences in the structure of our conscious and socially adjusted self. These repressed impulses are for Freud instinct-derivatives threatening to break into our ego from the unconscious and impersonal id, the inherited biological matrix of our natural organic needs. It has come to be recognized that this unconscious part of us plays a very large part in determining, not only neurosis and psychosis, but also criminal and delinquent behaviour, ordinary changes of mood, eccentricities, and even variations of personality-type in so-called normal persons. Apart from Freud's particular instinct theory, all this is now firmly established and generally accepted.

The important new developments concern the nature of this

unconscious inner region, this back-stage self which is so hard to get at but which is so well able to get at us. Moreover, it involves a new conception of the nature of mental life and the manner of its functioning and internal organization in the course of development. When we speak of a 'new' development we mean 'new' in a relative sense for no new development is an absolute break or sudden, totally unheralded, complete departure from what went before. The new grows at first within, and emerges out of the old. Just as Freud's own work developed out of hypnosis, so what has now come to be called 'object-relations theory' is not a break with Freud and a fresh start *de novo* along another line. It is a true development from Freud's own work, though it finally calls for a re-orientation of theoretical concepts. It arises in fact out of the most important inconsistency left unresolved in Freud's concepts, the contradiction we have already noted between the biological concept of instinct and the psychological concept of the super-ego.

Freud did not recognize that this theory of the super-ego necessitated a revision of his entire concept of psychic life as based on the theory of instincts. For Freud the human psyche is primarily impersonal, an id not an ego (an 'it' not an 'I'). He borrowed the term 'id' from Groddeck who held that we ought not to say '*we* live' but 'we are lived by the It', which is certainly a nihilistic theory so far as values are concerned. This id or 'it', the primary unconscious, is made up of impulses which are derivatives of biological instincts of sex and aggression. These instincts or 'id-impulses' are devoid of ethical sense and are not even personal for they are held to be there before the ego or personal self begins to develop. They are blind organic drives for piecemeal, bodily satisfactions or pleasurable discharge of physiological tension. The instincts are fundamentally unalterable; they can only be either *gratified* to make us anti-social, or *repressed* to make us neuroti-cally ill, or *tricked* into allowing their energies to be diverted to socially approved aims. This last, the theory of sublimation, is only open to the favoured few. Freud presented this dilemma uncompromisingly in his early paper on *Civilized Sexual Morality and Modern Nervousness* (*Collected Papers*, Vol. II, p. 76, 1908), and repeated it again and again, notably in *The Future of an Illusion* (1927) and *Civilization and its Discontents* (1930).

The ego and super-ego are, compared with the id, relatively superficial developments aiming to adjust id-impulses to outer reality. Thus our total psychic life consists for Freud of a controlling function struggling to allow to primarily impersonal biological instincts only so much gratification as is safe from the point of view of outer reality. This is really nothing but the age-old dualism of body and mind in modern psychological dress and contains no essential advance on traditional ideas: a disintegrating war of spirit against flesh.

It involves us in a biological fatalism and pessimism; man is the sport of his instincts which invade his superficial ego or familiar self from the impersonal organic substrate of his being. Man is the victim of his innate, and (for Freud) non-social, or anti-social, drives. Such a view undermines the sense of moral responsibility for oneself, for we cannot be held responsible for inherited factors over which we would never be able to establish more than a very precarious and unstable control.

Instinct theory, however, has in general come more and more to be challenged both in the academic and psycho-analytical spheres. American psychologists have largely discarded McDougall's idea of unitary, specific, instinctual drives. G. W. Allport regards all adult motivations as post-instinctual developments and as functioning autonomously (cf. *Personality*, 1937). C. S. Myers regarded instinct mainly as 'innate, directional determining tendency', i.e. *an inborn capacity to react in ways appropriate to the object or situation*. Modern academic psychology rejects the idea that '*specific* impulses' are innate and regards all actual impulses as called forth by the presenting object or situation of the moment, and as appropriate reactions to that object as the experiencing subject sees it. Thus the instinct of anger means not that we are endowed with a permanent specific impulse of aggression always seeking an outlet whether there is anything to be angry about or not, but rather that we have a latent inborn capacity to be angry when there is need so to react, as when we meet with frustration. *Instinct is potentiality and basic need, not specific impulse existing prior to experience.*

In the world of psychotherapy, American psychoanalysis of the school of Karen Horney and Erich Fromm, and psychiatrists of the school of Harry Stack Sullivan, have likewise discarded instincts in favour of dealing with *actual impulses as functions of human relationships*, as ways in which an individual reacts when integrated in a relationship with another individual or group. *Impulses do not exist apart from, and outside of, object-relations; and in fact, from the moment of conception in the womb no human being ever is outside of object-relationships. It is our very nature to be related to our environment, to which every psychic process is in some sense our reaction.* Thus in America there has been a widespread reorientation from a biological to a sociological point of view, giving priority to human relations over against instincts: a movement from thesis to anti-thesis. Psychoanalytically, however, this tends to superficiality, by having lost touch with the 'deep unconscious' of Freudian theory.

At this point the British contribution comes in, and represents a completion of the dialectical development. Fairbairn's 'object-relations theory' provides a synthesis of the Freudian deep unconscious and the emphasis on the psychological priority of human relationships in the shaping of our psychic life. It is equally true to say that Fairbairn provides a synthesis of the Freudian deep unconscious and Freud's own concern with object-relationships, on a fully psychological plane. For Freud was not by any means blind to the facts of object-relationships though he never produced a theory that gave them their proper place as the formative agencies in personality development. When Freud perceived that what is commonly called conscience consists in the setting up within the psyche of a mental replica of the child's parents as disciplinarian figures, and called this the super-ego, he created the concept of an 'internal psychic object', an object with which the ego sustains a persisting relationship, not in the outer world, but wholly inside the psyche itself. That is perhaps Freud's most original and far-reaching discovery and he ought, logically, to have followed it up into the depths of psychic life. Had he done so he would have discarded instinct theory as lying outside the properly psychological sphere; and he would have worked out a theory of psychic development in terms of the individual's reactions to and relations with, his objects, first external and then both internal and external. He did not take that step, but held to his original view that human development is determined by the organic maturation of libidinal instincts through oral, anal and genital stages.

It has fallen to Fairbairn to carry object-relations into the structure of the unconscious itself, and to show that *all our impulses can be understood only as reactions to objects, and that many of our impulses are reactions not to external objects but to objects that exist inside our very psychic make-up itself.* The *unconscious*, is to be understood not as a matrix of impersonal id-impulses, but as a *repressed inner world*, a continuous hidden drama of relationships between the ego and objects buried as it were within the psyche. This inner drama, with all the rôles played therein by both the ego and internal objects, perpetuates all of the life of childhood that the individual has been unable to outgrow. It is a perpetual living in a past which has been brought forward to constitute a secret, repressed, psychic present, so that we live outwardly in the present, and inwardly in the past at one and the same time.

This theoretical development by Fairbairn was made possible by the work of Melanie Klein who followed up Freud's super-ego theory, and elaborated it into a full scale theory of internal objects. The infant reacting to the ways in which he is dealt with by his parents, and projecting his own reactions on to them as well, mentally splits up the parent figures into a variety of whole and partial figures which he then introjects or takes into his own inner mental life. He thus becomes *mentally possessed* by a variety of objects to whom he goes on reacting with emotion, impulse and phantasy within himself. Fairbairn took the further step of recognizing that since the ego of the child is emotionally attached by his needs to all the aspects into which he divides up his parents in his own mind, *the splitting of the object involves also the splitting of the ego and the loss of the primary unity of psychic life*. From this come all psychopathological developments. Psychic life is now seen not as an apparatus of control over impersonal instinctual drives, but as a complex and highly personal drama throughout in its inner nature. *This personal drama of aspects of the ego and of objects in constant interaction constitutes the complex structure of the psychic individual.*

We may add that these theoretical developments have not come about as a result of armchair speculation but have been determined, like Freud's original views, by the need to understand the complex facts met with in clinical practice and the psychotherapeutic attempt to integrate minds in a state of internal conflict. To those familiar with religious literature and indeed cultural history in general, it will come as no surprise that human beings live a wholly 'interior life' within themselves as well as an external one. This neo-Freudian theory incidentally makes fully intelligible for the first time the 'split personality' phenomena first extensively studied by Morton Prince. For Fairbairn there is no mythical impersonal *id*; man is a whole self, an ego, and potentially a person from the start. The impulses and emotions we actually experience, chiefly longing for love, anger at frustration, fear of danger and guilt at disapproval are ways in which we react to other human beings. *Every impulse is the reaction of a subject to an object*. Actual impulses are determined, not by heredity, but by the situation. The important question is not what are you feeling but what are you reacting to, for it is only in the light of the person or situation one is reacting to that the nature of the reaction can be understood. It is, in a word, *not instincts but personal relationships which are the vital matter*. Our emotions are not functions of biological instincts but of human relations.

At this point the really revolutionary development arises.

Many people experience impulses, feelings and moods that bear no rational relationship to their actual visible situation in life. How can that be if emotion is a reaction to another person? A woman will say, 'I have the best of husbands yet I nag and lose my temper violently' or 'I've nothing to worry about yet I'm anxious and depressed all the time', or a man will say 'I'm happily married yet feel always sexually unsatisfied'. On the old theory all that could really be said was 'You've inherited an extra strong aggression or fear or sex instinct and that's that'—a hopeless view. Instead, we can now ask *'What is stimulating and keeping going your persistent anger or fear or sexual desire?* You are not reacting to *external* objects or situations (even though you sometimes think you are, and pin your reactions on to someone or other). *But you have another invisible inner world. Your unconscious is a whole world in itself peopled by beings with whom you have intense relationships of longing, anger and fear.* Who or what are you reacting to inside yourself?'

The unconscious is not a matrix of impersonal instincts but a world of persons whom we have taken into our minds and thrust out of consciousness along with parts of ourselves still tied to them and reacting to them. This can be seen quite clearly in dreams where it is not instincts but people we are troubled by. A middle-aged woman always feels afraid of doing the wrong thing, of making mistakes, and always feels guilty: why? She dreams that her father comes upstairs to her bedroom and thrashes her (as he used to do, though now he's been dead for years). There he is, an active person inside her mind, part of herself. A woman in the thirties who is irritable and intolerant of criticism and somewhat difficult to work with, dreams: 'there was mother on at me, nattering me as usual, telling me what to do and I turned on her at last and said "Shut up, I'll damn well please myself",' but this woman has for some years been living away from home. A man experiences a compulsive sexual and emotional craving for a woman: he dreams of chasing a woman who is always just out of reach and deserting him. He was deserted by his mother as a very small boy and passed on from one relative to another, unwanted; he is always hungry for a lost love he never recovers, but it is still going on inside his mind now, though he was not aware of it till he began to recognize the implications of his dreams.

All these highly disturbing personal relationships which belong primarily to the past, are perpetuated entire in the secret inner world of the unconscious. Part of our 'self', is locked away there with these 'bad internal objects' who perpetually arouse in us the troublesome angers, fears and hungry demanding needs that surge up to consciousness to disturb our outer life. *We live in two different worlds, external and material, internal and mental;* and our inner mental world is one we are not conscious of in a direct way but can only learn about by interpreting its indirect effects.

The unconscious is an unhappy world predominantly inhabited by figures who represent the frustrating aspects of our experiences of adults, and chiefly parents, when we were in our infancy and childhood. *The unconscious is a bad upsetting world because it is only that side of life we want to bury and forget.* Patients who have started by giving a quite idealized picture of their childhood, when they get talking and begin to remember the true state of affairs, will often break off and say, 'I don't want to talk about that, I want to forget it'. They do not realize that that policy keeps it alive inside, out of sight. *Where homes were really bad, the unconscious can be a real hell peopled by devils.*

But there is another reason why we keep alive inside us, and dream about, these bad upsetting figures. At bottom they represent parents and our troubles are due to the very intensity and strength of our emotional attachments. We would even feel guilty at letting them go. A little girl, asked if she would like to be taken away from a cruel mother to a kind one, said, 'No, I want my own Mummy.' If we were cold-blooded creatures incapable of emotional need and attachment we would suffer no psychoneurosis: we would be capable of anger if frustrated but it would be over and done with: we should know nothing about persisting hate, guilt, loneliness, anxiety or unhappiness.

All our troubles and sorrows arise out of our deep ineradicable need for love, for good-object relationships: our fundamental insecurities, fears, anxieties, angers and aggressions, and guilty feelings are all reactions to persons who have frustrated our love-needs, while we retain them and remain loyal to them deep down inside us, so that they go on upsetting us.

In our adult life sometimes these frustrating persons exist as real figures in our external world. We behave as bad-objects to each other and increase each other's insecurity. But so frequently that represents a *projection or externalization of situations we are involved in with aggravating, persecuting, frustrating and criticizing figures in our inner mental world.* One finds awkward, touchy, unreasonable, jealous, antagonistic people to cope with in all walks of life. It is difficult not to get impatient and feel that their behaviour is stupid and unrealistic. But why do they experience these 'irrational' reactions which they disconcertingly work out on the people around them. They are victims of unhappy past experiences from which they cannot get mentally free. Their emotions are not really a reaction to the outer scene at all in the first place. *They are in a state of subjective aggravation all the time because they are being 'got at' and upset by the people they live with inside themselves.* It is no good saying that people who only exist in one's mind are only imaginary persons. Psychologically they are powerful parts of ourselves and we suffer under them. A man wakes up with palpitating heart and drenched with sweat because his mother has been pouring out on him a torrent of angry moral abuse in his dream, though she has been dead twelve years. A man of fifty was sleeping in the afternoon, and half-waking, he saw his mother come in at the door to give him a thrashing. He actually burst out crying. In fact his mother had been dead twenty years but he was seeing her, and living with her in fear of her, in his mind. He projected her on to the actual figure of his wife who had come in to wake him with a cup of tea. Thus do human beings go on reliving their past life unconsciously, and getting it mixed up with the life of the present day. It is clear that here we have the true cause of those persisting undercurrents of mental pain or anxiety against which we need such powerful defences.

This leads us to the third reason for the retention of bad, frightening figures in our unconscious. We saw that in the first place we repress them, or banish them to the unconscious in order to get rid of them—at least from our conscious mental life. Then in the second place we remain emotionally attached to them however bad they are because they represent parents who were the sole objects of all our earliest libidinal needs.

But now a third reason for retaining them arises. They are both objects of our needs and desires (as parents) and at the same time frustrators of our needs and prohibitors of our desires (as rejective, angry, or disciplinarian authorities). Thus in the unconscious inner world we are forced to live in a state of tantalized, stimulated, excited needs which are never given any proper satisfaction. This perpetuates the outer situation of infancy in so far as the baby was allowed to get into a state of painful, unsatisfied, hungry craving through lack of proper emotional 'mothering'.

Starved needs grow more and more demanding, hungry and desperate. It is as if frustrated basic needs grow so intense, and are felt to the accompaniment of so much anger, that they are inwardly experienced as dangerous, devouring, biting, destroying impulses. Grave fears arise about expressing any needs at all lest they rush out with destructive violence. This terrible situation gives rise to the frequent neurotic fears of hurting, injuring or even killing the very people one most needs and loves. In fact when such aggravated primary need does break through unchecked to become a conscious characteristic, it leads to such demanding and possessive behaviour that the individual in question drains, exhausts, and wears out those upon whom he or she fastens. In the more pathological cases outbreaks of dangerous violence do occur.

We are faced then with the truly appalling fact that people can feel so full of dangerous tensions in body and mind when their fundamental human needs are too grossly thwarted from childhood onwards, that their main obsession is to stop themselves ever having the chance to release them in any active way. The personality must be kept inwardly in chains, inhibited, crushed into passivity, not allowed to be spontaneous in any way, but only allowed a very limited, circumscribed form of activity narrowly tied to duty. They do not feel safe unless they are under strict and powerful control. They cannot ever experience a happy *joie de vivre*. At best they can be gloomy saints of rigid character and usually censorious outlook. At worst they become progressively incapable of acting at all and fall victim to pathological states of melancholic depression or schizoid apathy. Suicide is the final, irrevocable act of self-suppression though it is also an indirect venting of anger against other people.

This crushing internal bondage and repression of all spontaneous vitality can be maintained by the retention of internal bad objects. There is less danger of outbreaks of dangerously strong needs, if a person lives in a state of unremitting anxiety and/or guilt aroused by persecuting figures in the unconscious, and projected into real people in the outer world. He feels surrounded by spies and policemen who will pounce on him if he is not careful. The third reason for the retention of internal bad objects is that they come to be needed as a means of controlling and suppressing the very starved, aggravated, angry needs of which they are the cause. In that state of mind one can know no peace: relaxation is impossible, wearing tension and conflict in body and mind is kept going by a persisting inner vicious circle of frustration, aggravation, repression, more frustration and so on. The situation within the personality and the strain engendered may, and often does, get worse as the years go by, leading to recurring nervous breakdowns. The personality has developed on the basis of an inherently self-frustrating pattern. Here is mental pain in its most chronic form and in all its grim, stark reality.

CHAPTER V

The Multi-personal Structure of Human Personality

WE have already mentioned the relatively simple view of the nature of human personality with which we all operate somewhat unreflectingly at the commonsense level of our ordinary conscious daily dealings with one another. It is assumed that human beings are single, simple, unified selves and react to each other as such. If we see something in another person that we either like or dislike strongly we hardly pause to question whether what we dislike and react to in him is really there. We see a person as this or that and take it for granted that he really is as we see him. We do not usually stop to ask 'Is what I am seeing really in him or is it in me; or, if it really is in him, does it affect me so much because it is in me also?'

We are familiar with the fact that other people can, as we say, *misunderstand* us, or see in us something we are certain is not in us at all. We explain it away by saying that they are prejudiced, have an axe to grind, or are careless and have not taken the trouble to know us properly. Sometimes they are right and are seeing what we are blind to. But sometimes they are wrong and are seeing only what they project into us. When they see us in some specially favourable light then we feel that, with some deductions on the ground of modesty, they are doing us justice, though in fact they may also be idealizing us to meet their own inner needs. In any case we do not as radically question our own judgments of other people as we do their judgments of us. We hardly stop to consider the astonishing extent and frequency of 'misunderstandings' in personal relationships even though we are familiar enough with them, nor do we very consistently realize the highly unrealistic ways in which people see and react to one another. Still less do we recognize what a challenge this is to our simple common sense views about human minds. People find it not merely disconcerting but even frightening to admit *how large is the subjective element in all our perceptions and judgments, i.e. how much of what we think we see is contributed by our own mental make-up.*

Novelists, no doubt, deal in such complexities of human experience and it does not disturb us much to read in a book about the troubles that arise because the fictitious characters, who to us are *other* persons, so lack the capacity to see each other in objectively real ways. In our own daily life in business and social intercourse we assume that our judgments are accurate or only limited by lack of sufficient knowledge of other people, and that, given adequate opportunity to know them, we can rely on ourselves always to see them as they really are. Our formula is: 'I am seeing him as he actually is, and I am a single unified person reacting to him as another single unified person.'

In reality, however, the whole situation is enormously more complicated. While this fact is obvious enough in everyday life to those who care to observe and reflect more carefully, it becomes especially clear in psychoanalytical treatment. The patient will say: 'I feel as if I am two different people, or even several different people; I am not consistent, I change so suddenly.' To match this the patient is just as likely to say to the analyst, 'I never know what you're going to be like. Every time I come you seem to me to be different.' It does not alter this fact that the patient may also be able to recognize intellectually, if not emotionally, that the analyst's attitude has a high degree of consistency and reliability. The formula has become: 'I am a group of different persons seeing and reacting to you who also seem to be a group of different persons, some of whom are probably really in you, and others of whom I project into you.'

This is the phenomenon discovered by Freud so early in his

work, and is one of his most epoch-making insights, technically called *transference*. The illustration of actual cases brings
cold theory to life. A common situation is the reliving, in
the setting of the analysis, of early strained relationships with
brothers and sisters. A patient who felt that I used an 'analytical knife' on him recalled how in childhood a violent-tempered
brother would seize a knife off the table at mealtimes and
attack him. Often a patient who is reacting to the analyst
during some particular session with open hostility and resistance, will insist that he is mocking, taunting, criticizing or
humiliating him. It may not be till after he has returned home,
or got to bed at night, that he will suddenly see himself as a
child again being mocked, taunted, teased, or humiliated by
an older brother or sister, and reacting either with tears or
temper, or else with a grim determination to control himself
and not say a word. This last reaction is very likely the one
he produced in session towards his analyst. The patient has
been seeing the persecuting brother or sister in the analyst,
so that everything the analyst does or says in session is made to
fit into the inner world pattern of the taunting siblings against
whom a defiant silent resistance has to be kept up.

But these hostile persecuting siblings have been built into
the patient's mental make-up and become active parts of his
own personality, and this has led to two further different
developments. The patient at times externalizes the situation
and reverses it, turning the tables on the analyst as he wished
to do in reality to his older brother long ago. Then it is the
analyst's turn to sit silent while the patient taunts him with
criticisms to the effect that psychoanalysis is no good or is
useless and destructive, or that he is no good as a psychotherapist and is only making the patient worse. Yet again the
patient will unwittingly play the rôle of the taunting, persecuting older brother or sister to himself. Here is a personality
that is not his own, but it exists as an active part of his own
personality-structure. He can project this alien personality
into other people and suffer under it, or he can identify himself with it, turn the tables and counter-attack, or finally, he

can keep the whole situation going inside himself and at one and the same time play the parts of both the persecuting sibling and his own suffering self.

A woman patient who in fact had an aggressive, violent-tempered, dominating mother, dreamed of her mother coming into her bedroom to murder her. Her main defence against this acute fear, and even terror, of her mother which she was always feeling in her unconscious inner world, lay in identifying herself with her mother. She would then rage in phantasy against all girl children and picture herself crushing and killing them. But again she would act out the whole tragic drama wholly inside herself, rage against herself and physically punch and beat herself. She would, moreover, project the hostile mother into older women in authority with whom she had to do, and then would fear and hate them in unrealistic ways, a fact which naturally made for very difficult and disturbed relationships in her work.

These cases, however, are only glaring examples of what is happening all the time in milder and less conspicuous ways with everybody. It is only by slowly and painfully gaining insight into this state of affairs that we can reduce our liability to such self-deceptions and unrealistic reactions. A milder case of this kind which I had the opportunity to investigate analytically was that of a young professional man. He sought analysis, not for a nervous illness, but for a lack of self-confidence which handicapped him in his work. He had a domineering father whose general attitudes were critical and depreciatory, who never spoke words of praise or appreciation to anyone, and who treated his son as a useless nincompoop who could not be trusted to do anything properly. The son automatically felt that all older men regarded him in the same way, and adopted apologetic attitudes to them, projecting into them the father who was a persisting factor in his own mind. But also he was conscious of a compulsion to treat both his equals and subordinates, and also himself, in the same way as his father treated him. He would find himself automatically behaving as if he were his father, and noted that he would criticize others but be quite unable to speak words of appreciation to them even when he wished to do so; and whenever he himself was about to embark on any activity he would sabotage his chances of success, and undermine his self-confidence, by carrying on a running fire of adverse, critical comment on himself. 'What's the good of you trying to do this, you're no good at this sort of thing, you'll only make a fool of yourself.'

There is a mutual psychic interpenetration of personalities in human relationships of a kind that can only be understood in the light of the personal histories of the persons related, from earliest childhood onwards. Some people are so dominated and overlaid by the personalities of their parents in their mental make-up, that they have never been able to develop any personality that could properly be called their own, a condition of most severe internal frustration.

The formula for personal relationships has now expanded into some such statement as this: 'I, plus mother, father, and a number of subsidiary figures who fuse together and are parts of my mental make-up, am seeing and reacting to another person who is similarly complex in make-up, and into whom I also project one or other or several of the figures in my inner psychic drama, usually without being at all aware that I am doing so.' The Rev. Bertram Smith, shrewd and famous pastor of Salem Congregational Church, Leeds, used to advise his young men: 'Before you marry a girl have a look at her mother.' His advice was more profoundly true and more far-reaching than he knew, and it can be generalized for all human relationships.

Dr. H. V. Dicks, in a study of *Experiences with Marital Tensions seen in the Psychological Clinic*, writes:

'A marital relationship (like any other) is a resultant of the interaction of forces inherent in two personalities with a long history, fashioned out of participation in past object-relationships, needs and pressures, from the cradle onwards, in the complex fields of their individual and social past. These histories provide the essential clues to the present structuring of their need systems, their values and their rôle-expectations. . . . We learn that people frequently love and marry not real persons, but that they in varying degree distort the reality by investing their objects with qualities from past significant psychological objects, among whom parents of the opposite or even of the same sex are common.' (*Brit. J. of Med. Psych.*, Vol. XXVI, Pts. 3 and 4, 1953, pp. 183 and 186.)

It will be well to pause and take stock at this point. Some readers may well feel somewhat overpowered by this picture of the complexity of human personality and therefore of human relationships. They may well feel discouraged and somewhat pessimistic and hopeless about the solving of human problems in the face of such facts. That check to easy optimism may, in a sense, be salutary and much needed. Preachers are open to the temptation to oversimplify human problems by the too glib use of magic words like 'faith' and 'trust in God'. The intractable nature of political and international suspicions, hates and rivalries, which cannot all be explained as due to economic and geographical pressures, should warn us against shallow optimism based on too simple views of human nature. The problems of widespread marital disharmony and divorce, of delinquency and crime, and many chronically persisting social evils should give pause to our natural desire to see things as less complex than they really are. Wishful thinking is no basis for individual and social betterment. Unnecessary discouragement over the slender results of years of preaching, religious ministration, educational advance, and social reform may be avoided by facing boldly the real complexity, psychologically, of all human relationships and problems.

But we must add that the facts here set forth concerning the multipersonal structure of human personality do not constitute an unrelieved picture of a morbid and inevitably pathological state of the human mind. *Fundamentally, this fact that the human individual incorporates into his personality in the process of growing up, much of the personalities of the significant*

*people who preside over his formative years, is the natural condition
of human development.* If it can work evil, it can also work
good. Not every child is doomed to incorporate parents of
such a depressing and destructive type as to be unable thereafter to grow into a happy, stable, and mature adult. That
this is the fate of far too many children is proved by the widespread prevalence of actual neurosis, and by the large numbers
of inhibited, nervous, shy, restricted or difficult personalities
to be met with. How many people can be said to have
developed to anything like their full natural capacity?

Dr. J. D. Sutherland, writing on *Psychological Medicine and
the National Health Service*, says:

'For the psychoneuroses and the character disorders the
existing facilities over the country as a whole for other than
palliative treatment are almost negligible in face of the size
of the needs. . . . A little reflection on the scale and cost of
psychological illness is salutary.

(i) In England and Wales there are approximately 150,000
people in mental hospitals.

(ii) Russell Fraser (1947) and his colleagues showed that
approximately 10 per cent of the industrial population had
suffered from definite and disabling neurotic difficulties,
and a further 20 per cent from minor forms of neurosis. . . .
Neurotic illness caused between a quarter and third of all
absence from work due to illness; neurosis caused more
absence than colds and influenza. Of the total available
working days, 1 per cent in the case of men and 2.4 per cent
in the case of women are lost annually from psychological
illness.

(iii) Such estimates as exist would tend to show that
about a third of most general practitioners' work is concerned
with illness in which the psychological factor is prominent.

The human suffering that this represents gives ample
reasons for serious efforts. But if, in addition, we reckon
the cost of these disorders, both the direct cost of their
treatment and the indirect cost in the loss of productivity,

a conservative estimate of the national bill for psychological disorder must be £100 m. per annum. It would therefore appear that the need to take effective therapeutic and preventive action is urgent.' (*Brit. J. of Med. Psych.*, Vol. XXV, Pts. 2 and 3, 1952, p. 71.)

On the other hand, wherever the child has friendly, loving, tolerant and wise parents, and particularly parents who respect the child's own individuality and seek to discover and foster what he, himself, is rather than force on him some pattern of their choice, that child will have incorporated parent-figures who are an abiding source of inner strength, and who, by reason of their encouraging and stimulating attitudes to the child, enable him to develop a genuine personality of his own without fear or guilt. The tragedy of the situation is that disturbed parents send forth disturbed children to become in their turn the disturbed parents of yet another disturbed generation. This is a vicious circle that is very hard to break. But human beings *are* open to healing influences, and all the more so when they become accurately acquainted with the inner nature of the personality-problems to be solved.

We are here, for the moment, more specifically concerned with the light which modern psychological knowledge sheds on mental pain, so that we need not apologize for concentrating chiefly on the dark side of the picture. That there is another side we shall see when we take up the question of 'cure'. Meanwhile we need not discourage ourselves when we look closely into the facts which show more plainly than ever the overwhelming importance of good parental influence for the growth of sound personality in the child.

Fairbairn has reduced the apparent confusion and complexity of what we have called the multi-personal structure of human personality by laying bare the basic pattern to which these phenomena conform, in spite of individual and family differences. He shows reason to believe that there is *a basic endopsychic situation, a fundamental structural pattern of human personality*, evolved in the course of development, which is the same for everyone in broad outline. It is an organizational framework within which the infinite variety of individual differences exists.

The psyche of the newborn babe, prior to the play of environmental influences upon it, is characterized by a pristine unity. He is a single unified subject reacting with needs to, and experiencing satisfactions both bodily and emotional from, his primary object, the maternal breast: even though as yet he is incapable of distinguishing between subject and object in his experience. If the infant's experience could remain one of uninterrupted satisfactions and good relationships with his object-world, he would retain his inner psychic unity or wholeness. But that is a manifest impossibility. Only inside the womb if anywhere is undisturbed satisfaction possible. After birth the infant begins to encounter not only pleasurable experiences of satisfied needs and a secure relationship to the nursing-mother, but also frustrations, disappointments, denials, frightening experiences. He reacts with increasingly complex emotional oscillations of pleasure, need, and desire, anxiety, fear, frustration-rage and aggression. The peaceful unity of his psychic life is disrupted by conflicts of feeling and impulse. *He cannot retain inner unity and consistency in face of the disunity and inconsistency of his outer world. Processes are set in motion which result in a splitting of his ego in and by the diverse and contradictory object-relationships in which he is involved.* These begin with mother and expand to take in the father, siblings, and in time an ever increasing number of extra-familial figures. But before that stage is reached his experience with the parents will already have laid down the ground-plan of his mental organization, upon which all later experience will be built up. The splitting of the ego, entailing as it does the loss of spiritual integrity of the person, becomes permanently established by repression very early in life. It may be to some extent modified spontaneously by later favourable experience and an improving relationship with parents through childhood to the end of adolescence. After that it will not prove amenable to any fundamental change. Later experience can shift the balance of power inside the unaltered pattern. Religious experiences, experiences in human relationships, and psycho-analytical therapy can, as it were, drain mental energy out of some aspects of the total psychic structure and divert it to or reinforce it in others; but one's basic experience in life in the mouldable years of childhood is what it is and leaves permanent results on the developing psyche.

Certain definite principles appear to operate universally in human experience. The simplest and most obvious is that the child will seek to retain good and satisfying objects and experiences, and rid himself of bad ones. So far as we are able we all seek to do this throughout life, and as adults we certainly have greater scope for choice and liberty of action than the baby has. We can, at least to some extent and sometimes, get away from people and circumstances we do not like and associate with those we can be happy with. The infant has no power of choice or freedom of action at all in this matter. Whatever his parents and home are like he must put up with the situation and cannot in any way change it. *His only method of protecting himself against painful experiences is by means of what we might call mental tricks.* He can do nothing at all about his outside world; he is in its power. He can, however, even though in blind and automatic ways, do something to alter his internal mental world. Thus arise mental events that are destined to dominate his entire future development.

The process of holding on to the good and trying to get rid of the bad becomes a process technically known as the idealization of the external object and the mental incorporation, introjection or internalization, and repression of the bad object. The child, in his need to keep his outer world (primarily his parents) good in his eyes, splits his mental image of them into two parts, a good image and a bad image. The bad image, i.e. much of his experience of parents in their depriving, frustrating and frightening capacity, he then represses or makes unconscious. The good image is projected on to the actual outer parent whose difficult aspects are then ignored. The results of this at a later stage can be seen in the child who cannot admit that anything is wrong with one or both of his parents but who in sleep is persecuted in nightmare dreams by terrifying figures who are in fact the emotionally bad side of the same parents. Once the image of a bad, persecuting figure is lodged firmly in the child's mind he is predisposed apprehensively to find such a bad figure repeatedly in real life, and often in order to retain both parents as good figures he will fasten on some neighbour, schoolteacher or distant relative on whom to project the bad object.

Yet another manoeuvre is illustrated by a patient for whom both parents were very considerably bad objects in reality. The father was a violent tempered man and the mother an excessively dominating woman. The child was forced many times to listen to frightening quarrels between her parents from her earliest years onwards. The resulting situation in which the child became afraid of both parents was emotionally insupportable and the child hit on what was probably the only possible solution open to her. She elected to regard her father as the bad object and her mother as the good object. All her fear, hate and rejection became centred upon her father. In him she hated all that was bad to her in both parents. Then in order to gain some basic security in life she turned wholly to her mother, took her side in all the quarrels, and by becoming totally submissive to her she succeeded in keeping her mother as a wholly good figure. She grew up believing that she loved her mother devotedly, having entirely blotted out from consciousness all the resentment she felt at the ruthless way her mother suppressed all independence and individuality in her. But she also grew up to fall increasingly a victim to both hysteric and psychosomatic illness, which was caused by the hidden working in her of all the anger and aggression she could not openly express against her tyrant protectress. It took a very long analysis before she could bear to let herself become aware once more of the fact that the terrifying events of her early life had built up in her a tremendous hate of her mother as well. Not till then did it become possible for her even to get a chance of dealing with this on an adult level, and outgrowing the bad effects of her early development. But meanwhile many years of her adult life had been largely wasted in the struggle with neurosis, and her personality had been all but crippled.

Thus the child comes to see one or other, if not both, of his outer real parents as better than they are, and unconsciously experience his inner, repressed, mental versions of them as worse than they are. He has split the unity of his objects and in doing so splits the unity of his own ego, for he remains emotionally attached to both good and bad objects. In repressing the bad objects into the unconscious he must split off and repress (and therefore lose from consciousness) parts of himself as well.

Thus all of us, in varying degrees, store up and preserve unconsciously in our minds precisely what has most upset us and made us unhappy in our past life, and especially our early past. According as it was very bad or not so bad, according as the important people who early shaped and determined our lives were really hard, loveless, domineering, bad tempered, frightening, or else were milder and more helpful figures, so is our inner world. But our unconscious picture of the parents of our childhood is always much worse than our conscious idealized memory of them. *We carry about with us, and secretly live in, a bad inner world which in some cases may be a veritable hell. The more disturbed and unstable people are, the more virulent does their inner hell turn out to be*, and the more they will be found to suffer from persecutory or depressive anxiety within themselves. The milder the inner world is, the more stable, mature and normal the person is able to be. But *to some extent, varying from person to person, all human beings live with a part of themselves shut up or imprisoned in a secret unconscious mental world where they feel unloved, unvalued, unwanted, rejected, frustrated, blamed, condemned: and therefore frightened, lonely, insecure, angry and enraged, and guilty.* It is in this region of the mind that mental pain has its deepest causes. Further there can be little doubt that here we have a clear view of those facts about human nature that caused the religious dogmas of Hell and original sin to arise.

All this conflicting mass of emotion and impulse surges up to consciousness ever and anon to upset relationships in the outer world. One of the tragic things to a psychoanalyst is to have to watch patients upsetting their own children in exactly the same way as their parents upset them in the past, and still go on upsetting them inside. For the early experience creates parent-child patterns of relationship which tend automatically to reproduce themselves when the child in turn becomes a parent. We tend to sentimentalize and idealize parenthood but the grim plain fact is that we cannot be any more mature as parents than we are as persons, and even when we try not to do so we automatically reproduce in our handling of our children a good deal of what was emotionally unsatisfactory in the way our parents handled us—just as, in their turn, our parents were similarly tied to their parents. These facts give us a new interpretation of the Old Testament text, 'The sins of the fathers shall be visited on the children even unto the third and fourth generation.' Children often grow up to be intellectually more enlightened than their parents were, but even then they remain much more on their parents' level emotionally than they recognize. We can be reasonable so long as all is going well. As soon as situations arise which generate emotional tensions we begin to regress to the primitive emotional patterns of parent-child relationships which are embedded in the unconscious structure of our personality, which have perpetuated the least mature aspects of our parents' dealings with us in our childhood.

It is quite common to find that children are afraid of their parents, feel not understood by parents, and seldom take their parents into their confidence. This does not necessarily mean that their parents are definitely bad types. In any case it would get us nowhere simply to blame parents, for they in turn are what they are because of the difficulties they encountered in their own childhood. But many parents who are excellent people in a general way have little imaginative capacity to understand what impressions they are making on the minds of their children. They often show a singular aptitude for irritating and exasperating their children quite unnecessarily. Dr. H. V. Dicks writes: 'People will fail in marriage when they are apparently well adapted in all other social rôles.' (op. cit. p. 182.) But this is even more true of parenthood. People can fail as parents even when they succeed as marriage partners.

Recently I was helping a patient to work her way out of quite serious timidities in meeting other people. She spoke of her parents to whom she was very devoted, but recollected that as a child she was definitely afraid of her mother's raised voice and her father's stern look. She went on to speak of her childhood fears of the dark, of faces she saw in the dark, and of her one great besetting fear of rag-and-bone men. She was always sure they would put her in their sack and take her away. About that time, it so chanced that on a train journey I shared a compartment with a mother, father and small boy of about three years. They impressed me as sensible people with a good relationship to each other and to the child. In particular a happy, affectionate relationship existed between father and son, though the boy cuddled up quite happily to his mother when he got tired. The journey, however, tried him and he got restless, whereupon his mother said, 'If you're not good a man will come and take you away'. Just then the engine emitted a shrill whistle and the child started and looked frightened. The father said, 'There, that happened because you're not a good boy'. Later on, in moving around, the boy put his hand on my knee and the father said, 'Take your hand off the gentleman's knee. If you do that he'll pick you up and carry you away'. The child darted a quick scared glance at me and was not wholly reassured by my smile. I thought of my patient's fears of rag-and-bone men and of meeting strangers. In a multitude of such ways the security of children is preyed upon by the unimaginative folly of adults who have little idea of how sensitive a receptor is the child's mind. The child acquires a gallery of frightening figures compounded partly of disturbing aspects of parents, partly of terrors elaborated by an anxious imagination, and partly also of the child's own repressed angers. The whole is buried by repression in the course of growing up to form a permanent hidden fifth column within the adult mind, while grown-ups naïvely suppose the child is growing out of its early fears. Later the psychoanalyst finds them lurking behind the symptoms of neurosis and emerging in dreams.

Fairbairn, we mentioned, has reduced to its basic simplicity the pattern of internalized bad objects and of the consequent splitting of the ego. From the child's point of view the parents have, broadly speaking, three major aspects, the affectionate (libidinal), the angry (aggressive), and the educative and disciplinarian (moral) aspects. At one moment the mother in the train put her arm round the little boy and cuddled him up to her and he snuggled close to her body; at another she smacked him and when, naturally following her example, he hit back with a small clenched fist she smacked him harder and made him cry: yet again she promised him that if he were a good boy he would have some sweeties when they got home, but she threatened him with 'the man who would take him away' if he were naughty (prototype of the God who sends sinners to Hell).

The affectionate parent is libidinally exciting, that is to say arouses the child's desire (libido) to be loved, comforted, caressed and to enjoy bodily intimacies with mother, and also to be valued, understood, and to be the recipient of genuine interest. In being thus loved the child learns to give love as well as to receive it. All aspects of the child's future love life, sexual, emotional and personal, will have their earliest roots in this relationship, which will unconsciously impose its dominant pattern on them. *The aggressive parent is libidinally rejective*, that is to say spurns the child's advances, crossly threatens, attacks and frightens him, and arouses in him an answering anger which, in its expressions, tends to be modelled on that of the parent. The child wants to smack the parent who smacks him and rejects the parent who rejects him, till fear makes him lock up his anger inside and even turn it against himself so that he becomes inhibited, passive, and develops the basis for obsessional, hysteric or psychosomatic illness. All aspects of the child's future aggressive feeling and behaviour, and also of his timid and nervous behaviour, have their roots here. *The moral and educative parent is libidinally satisfying only on condition of the child's obedience and submissiveness, and gives love mainly in the form of approval.* The moral parent is the starting point of the child's ego-ideal, but along with the aggressive parent is the origin of the child's conscience or super-ego which may be quite harsh and tyrannical.

With a well-balanced parent in whom a genuine and sensibly demonstrative affection combines with a minimal tendency to personal aggressiveness and reasonable moral and educational standards and demands, the child can grow up with a relatively small amount of object-splitting and ego-splitting. But many parents, because of their own personality problems, have little capacity for demonstrative affection and even a distaste for it, while they fall easily into angry outbursts and are harsh and condemnatory in their discipline. One woman patient who had been exceptionally love-starved in childhood, and who had grown up to stifle all her personal needs in a detached and cold personality, reported not only that her husband said she froze him off, but also that, as treatment proceeded, she one day suddenly felt that she was fond of her small daughter. Her immediate reaction was to feel cross and stifle her emotions again. Thus a fearful inability to love is transmitted from one generation to another.

The child's need for love grows more and more starved, hungry, frustrated and angry; and his counter-aggression against, yet fear of, the parent grows more and more disturbing. He will, unless he becomes frankly a problem child, seek safety in trying to maintain as tolerable a relationship as may be on the basis of compliant obedience to the disciplinary parent. Thus he at least averts a fair amount of anger. His general tendency is likely to become that of keeping on the right side of mother and father, and splitting off and repressing both his hunger for love and his resentful aggression, even though these may break through at times if only in some such symptoms as bed-wetting or bad dreams. If his anger shows more openly it is likely to meet with a hostile reception from the parents who probably have little patience with the child's needs and moods, and mainly desire that he shall not be a nuisance. A child of such parents can grow but little assured sense of his own value, and will be seriously inhibited in his capacity to love and to sustain good and healthy relationships with other people.

In order to simplify the situation and control the development of anxiety, the parents are split in the child's mind into three separate parent-images, two of whom become fairly effectively repressed into the unconscious. Likewise the child, by reason of his attachment to the parents and need of them, becomes himself split into three distinct egos, two of which are repressed along with the parent-figures appropriate to them. *The unity of the personality is split in a threefold way.* Using Fairbairn's terminology, the *Central Ego*, the part of the child's personality which remains conscious and preconscious, is tied in an obedient, approved relationship to the parents as *Ideal Objects*. The frightened but also angry and resentful aspect of himself is repressed to form an unconscious subsidiary ego called by Fairbairn the *Anti-libidinal Ego* tied mainly by identification to the repressed aggressive parent-image, the *Rejecting Object*. This unconscious anti-libidinal self functions, as Fairbairn denoted in his earlier name for it, as an *Internal Saboteur*; it is a part of himself that has turned against his own needs out of fear of parental disapproval, and sabotages all his active, spontaneous, creative self-expression. *The Libidinal Ego*, or the needy child craving for love, is repressed along with the tantalizing, depriving, though libidinally exciting parent, the *Exciting Object*.

Thus in his conscious relationships with the outer world the child grows up to be, in varying degrees, modelled on the parents' emotional pattern. He conforms to social expectations but with a personality impoverished by the loss of much of its capacity for vigorous affectionate-sexual and also normally self-assertive reactions. Meanwhile in the unconscious the repressed and disowned parts of himself live in a world of perpetual love-starvation, fear and aggression. The basic pattern of the inner structural organization of the personality, conscious and unconscious, is threefold.

1. Conscious.   The *Central Ego* related to the *Ideal Object* (approving parent).

2. Unconscious.   The *Anti-Libidinal Ego* related to the *Rejecting Object* (aggressive parent).

3.   „   The *Libidinal Ego* related to the *Exciting Object* (desired parent).

The complexity of personality is seen to lie in the fact that, owing to early processes of psychic splitting,

1. There are three relatively distinct selves.

2. There are three relatively distinct internalized personal objects.

3. In course of time other external objects, siblings, acquaintances, teachers, workmates, bosses, friends and enemies, contribute to the mental elaboration of the three basic internal objects.

4. This leads to parallel developments in the three ego-structures.

5. A constant mutual and reciprocal interaction goes on between this inner psychic world and the outer world of everyday life.

The most striking feature of all this is that *the complex development of human personality stems from the wellnigh unbreakable strength of the child's primary emotional attachment to his parents, on all sides of their own complex make-up*. The better they are as parents, the more stable is his personality. But however unsatisfactory they may be, the child seems to be incapable of giving them up in his inner mental life.

To all outer appearance the child's aim in growing up is to become independent of parents. But that is made up for internally by a strong and intense attachment, so intense an attachment that what grows into us as children can never really be got out of us again. It permanently conditions our character and personality. Psychoanalysts are sceptical of the possibility of fundamentally altering the basic structure of a personality once it has taken shape and become consolidated after adolescence, even though important changes in its mode of functioning can be made. The difficulty lies, it seems, in the astonishing tenacity of our emotional adhesion to our first love-objects, though there is always the possibility that early emotional development may be registered in and consolidated in early physiological development. At any rate, psychologically, we may say that *our major problems are caused by our unshakable primary emotional loyalties. Deep down we never desert entirely those who gave us birth and brought us up.* We retain as conscious memory the pleasing side of our experience of them, and use it to idealize the picture. The other side, where we felt misunderstood, lonely, criticized, undermined in our self-confidence, resentful at frustrating controls and interferences, is largely repressed. We may remember some of this, but we bury the worst, not as memory, but as an actual living, continuing relationship with menacing figures going on and on in this inner world which we only occasionally catch sight of in dreams. It is the source of anxiety and mental pain.

A final brief word must be said about conscience, or the Freudian super-ego. Freud held that it is simply a mental replica of the morally disciplinarian parent, a single internal psychic object. Fairbairn's analysis shows that it is much more complex. He resolves it into three components. It comprises within itself the Ideal Object and the Ego Ideal, the Rejecting Object, and the Anti-Libidinal Ego. The idealized parent adopted as our own ego ideal, because of our need as children to maintain as good a relationship with our actual parents as we can, constitutes the most conscious part of our complex conscience. It is the part that is accessible to normal educational influences. If it is not too much interfered with and dominated by the unconscious parts, it can become the basis of a developing, maturing, progressive, rational morality.

The Rejecting Object (the angry, punitive parent) and the Anti-Libidinal Ego (or Internal Saboteur, the part of our own ego attached to and modelled on the Rejecting Object) constitute the unconscious or repressed parts of our conscience. They are the source of all the harsh, self-destructive operations of a pathological conscience which causes neurotic guilt and fear, and in extreme cases the morbid states of depression and anxiety. Rational guilt is a reaction of sorrow and shame over a specific wrong actually committed. Morbid depressive and persecutory guilt is guilt not over actual deeds but over deeds done in unconscious phantasy, over sins of thought and feeling only. It is a persisting reaction to a persisting internal danger, namely the outbreak of violently aggravated unconscious needs. Morbid guilt is an unremitting self-attack designed to forestall the commission of specific anti-social acts by crushing out all free and spontaneous vital activity. It is as if it aims to prevent our doing wrong by preventing our doing anything at all, and it can, in melancholia, reduce the personality to total immobility. But in a deeper sense it aims to perpetuate the repression of our internal bad objects, as if it were aroused by a sense of our keeping bad company in the unconscious. It involves a turning against ourselves, at deep psychic levels, of the aggression we feel against the emotionally bad side of parents. The anti-libidinal ego is a part of ourselves in which we have 'gone over to the enemy' and turned against ourselves. It can be recognized in active operation in people who betray a compulsion to be for ever depreciating and depriving themselves, undermining their own self-confidence and spoiling all their pleasures and satisfactions in life. It is not difficult to find people who literally give themselves no peace and seem quite incapable of allowing themselves to enjoy any constructive activity. One patient said 'Everything I want to do I stop myself doing it. I don't know how I do this but I know I do do it.'

The mental pain which we are seeking to understand always contains a large amount of unconsciously motivated self-punishment, self-attack and self-torture, which the sufferer cannot recognize for what it is. It is apparent then that human personality, in and through the threefold splitting processes described, may be seen as functioning according to *a fundamentally dualistic and self-frustrating pattern*. This has been recognized since the early ages of man's self-reflection. A dualistic account of man can be traced through Greek philosophy and Persian religion, Roman Stoicism and the Oriental Mystery Religions, to the Christian religion, especially in the Pauline doctrine of the inevitable war between the law of the mind and the law of the members. This radical dualism has usually been represented in varying ways as an antagonism of body versus mind. Freud took over this traditional view in the theory of an inherited instinctual Id rooted in the body and opposed to and by a mentally developed ego and super-ego. Freud, however, came finally to represent this antagonistic dualism in human nature as itself innate, when he put forth the theory that libido and aggression were manifestations of innate life and death instincts. The impulse to live, to love, to unite, to reproduce is, he taught, always opposed and counter-attacked in us by an equally innate and ultimate urge towards death, hate, division and destruction. This theory of a 'Death Instinct' proved to be one of the most widely questioned and rejected of all Freud's views, even among psychoanalysts. However, this long and unbroken line of evidence for man's feeling that a radical dualism of an antagonistic kind existed in his nature, and that it works in self-destructive ways, poses a problem that calls for solution.

Fairbairn's formulation of the problem seems to the present writer to be the most satisfactory one to date. For him *the dualism consists of a libidinal factor and an anti-libidinal factor opposed to one another in our internal psychic economy*, but he regards it as a developmental, not an innate, phenomenon. This appears in his use of the terms 'Libidinal Ego' and 'Anti-Libidinal Ego' for the secondary, repressed personalities that develop in us. The Central Ego, according to the character of the parents, in their idealized aspect, will tend either in the libidinal or the anti-libidinal direction. The anti-libidinal factor is aggression, and in whatsoever way, and to whatsoever extent, anger, aggression and hate (reactions to frustration) persist actively in a personality, to that extent all its natural impulses towards living, loving, and being spontaneously active and creative (in sexual, vocational, artistic and intellectual ways) will be inwardly opposed and inhibited by counter-tendencies of a hostile, hating and destructive kind. Guilt and anxiety over the release of aggression against external objects (in the beginning parents) cause us to turn our aggression against ourselves and take the side of those who frustrate us. As one patient put it: 'All my life I have given myself a bad time. If I hadn't I would have given others a bad time.' Another patient says: 'When I feel angry I feel someone has got to be hit and it had better be me,' so she shuts herself in her room and punches her own body. Such indiscriminate self-attack undermines people in their dealings with others and steadily weakens their own personality.

The reversal of aggression into self-attack, however, more usually becomes repressed and goes on unconsciously in dangerously self-destructive forms. It is the cause in the long run of all the crippling bodily illnesses of an hysteric and psychosomatic order, and of all equally crippling mental states of morbid guilt, anxiety, inferiority, nervousness, and inhibition. *This anti-libidinal factor of inturned aggression constitutes a perpetual secret campaign of internal sabotage of the personality* which, as we saw at the end of chapters three and four, *involves the functioning of the personality on an inherently self-frustrating pattern. This is undoubtedly the ultimate internal cause of mental pain*, and it is the ultimate psychic dualism in human nature, albeit a dualism not of an innate but of a developmental order.

Part II.

MENTAL DEFENCES

CHAPTER VI

The Primary Defences Against Anxiety

IN Part I we have explored the fact and nature of mental pain. We have seen that this involves much more than occasional feelings of fear, anxiety, grief and frustration concerning actual disturbing events in the outer world of the present day. By far the greater and most important part of the mental pain suffered by human beings has its causes internally, even though this ultimately reflects and perpetuates the externally caused pains of the past. It arises now out of the very mental make-up or 'endopsychic structure' of individual personalities. We saw how, as a result of early difficulties in personal relationships in the home, the infant and small child undergoes mental developments of a kind which actually keep alive those difficulties in an exaggerated form as a fundamental, though unconscious and repressed, part of his growing personality-structure. By reason of this, mental pain in its two basic forms, persecutory and depressive anxiety, is continually 'manufactured', as it were, in the unconscious throughout life, both in association with and also independently of difficulties in the outer environment. In fact a person's ability to stand up to external difficulties depends largely on the degree of anxiety embedded in his mental make-up at deep levels. It is this state of affairs that is so often popularly expressed in such statements as 'If she hasn't got any worries she has to invent some' or 'He's a great worrier, always looking for trouble.' Such people are repeatedly advised to stop worrying but their tragedy is that they cannot. The unremitting production of anxiety is actually an inescapable function of their personality by reason of the way it was shaped by the circumstances of their early formative years. They can only stop being anxious by means of some psychotherapeutic process of re-development that enables them to undergo important changes, if not in the ground-plan of their psychic make-up, then at least in the way they function in their dealings with the outer world. For their personalities are working on a self-frustrating pattern according to which aggression is turned inwards to operate as an anti-libidinal, inhibiting and life-destroying factor.

Meanwhile, as we may say, 'nature' experiments on its own to find ways and means of dealing with, eliminating, immobilizing, or controlling this dangerous anxiety of internal origin, and the aggression that gives rise to it. It appears that there are certain stock methods of setting up internal psychic defences against this menace from within the mind itself. So far as we can see they are sufficiently limited in number for psychoanalytical investigation to discover them all; and also they appear to be universal, to arise spontaneously in individuals of every age, past and present, of every culture, and of every locality and race. The more we deal with the conscious social self, the more we find that individuals differ; the deeper we get into the unconscious foundations of the personality, the more similarity do we find. The basic dynamics of the human psyche appear to be constant, and they consistently underlie the greatest possible variety in individual and cultural development. Schizoid and depressed personalities, hysteric, paranoid, obsessional and phobic reaction-types, may be discerned alike in primitive and modern men, and in human beings of all civilizations and creeds.

There is no evidence that 'human nature' undergoes any radical change as to its major modes of development and functioning. There is, of course, plenty of evidence that the natural psychic defences against internal anxiety vary greatly in the success they achieve in different individuals, and that they operate variously in different cultural settings. There is also evidence that the basic internal anxiety-situation can be modified favourably by therapeutic measures of a religious, social and psychological kind; though no one pretends that this is easy, and therapeutic optimism is soon checked by realism when we try to 'remake broken lives'. In this Part II, however, we are concerned to study these spontaneously arising psychic defences against mental pain, in the absence of therapeutic endeavours, i.e. the ways in which the individual psyche strives alone and within itself to achieve and maintain sufficient emotional stability to be able to cope with the outer environment in daily living. In Part III we shall turn to the problem of 'cure or therapy'.

It is well to remind ourselves that there are two sources of anxiety and two dangers against which defences are needed, first the existence of disturbing bad objects in the unconscious (inside the mind) and second the existence of the violent emotions and impulses they arouse which may be discharged upon external objects. The individual is worried about losing control of sexual and aggressive impulses and behaving in an anti-social manner, i.e. about reacting to the outer world with emotions that arise in and really belong to the inner one. Freud concerned himself solely with anxiety about impulses and he regarded repression as aimed fundamentally against impulses or instinct-derivatives. This was the inevitable starting-point for the study of the problem, since the impulses emerge into consciousness while the internal bad objects that arouse them are hidden in the unconscious and have taken a long time to discover.

Fairbairn has now shown, however, that Melanie Klein's discoveries concerning internal objects make it plain that what are primarily repressed are bad objects, and that the repression of bad impulses is secondary to, and a result of, the repression of the bad objects that arouse them. If bad objects can be got rid of, bad impulses will not occur in the absence of external provocation, for they arise out of the feelings bad objects evoke in us. Inability to control our emotions is rooted in inability to control or master the bad objects that arouse them. If we could stop bad objects frustrating or goading us, we would solve the problem of the control of impulse and emotion. That is what we try to do when our persecutors are in the external world, by attack, persuasion or flight. But as Freud repeatedly stressed one cannot take flight from internal dangers, and this observation is more telling when we remember that these internal dangers are not simply anti-social impulses, as Freud believed, but persecutors lodged within the mind itself.

The danger we really fear, when we become anxious about breaking out into anti-social behaviour, is the danger of suddenly seeing real people as the reincarnations of our original and now internal, repressed bad objects, and of reacting to them in that light. This is the danger of automatic and unwitting projection of our inner world into our outer one, causing a distortion of our perception of outer reality. It will be useful to keep in mind this distinction between danger from bad objects and from bad impulses, while recognizing that they cannot in fact be separated for the latter depends on the former. They are really all one phenomenon.

To illustrate this fact of bad feelings arising as a reaction to the projection of an internal bad object into an actually present outer person, I may mention a striking example of a patient suddenly experiencing a negative transference to me. During the course of one session I gave her a friendly smile and she at once became very frightened. I asked why and she said she was afraid because she felt a sudden surge of hatred for me when I smiled. To my enquiry as to whether she had any idea why my smile should arouse hate in her, she replied that it looked to her a sinister smile and made her feel I was dangerous. I asked her if she could say what this 'sinister smile' made her think of. At once she said: 'Father: whenever he was going to beat me, that horrible sinister smile would come over his face first. It terrified me.' Freud discovered that patients transfer on to the analyst the feelings they had towards parents. But now it appears that a deeper phenomenon is involved. *The transference of emotion only happens as a result o, the projection of an internal bad object.* The sinister smiling face of her aggressive father was a persisting bad object in the mind of this patient. So long as this internal bad object was not involved, this patient could react to me in a friendly way and seek my help. As soon as something prompted her to project this internal bad object on to me, she at once began to react to me as if I were her sinister smiling, dangerously bad-tempered father. The re-appearance in me of a bad object of her childhood, and the arousal in herself of violent emotions of fear and hate were but two aspects of the same phenomenon, one which caused her to experience a very marked anxiety attack. These are the dangers against which psychic defences are spontaneously built up in the course of mental development. Every effort has to be made to suppress internal bad objects and the emotions and impulses they arouse, in order to make life in the outer world possible.

One defensive manoeuvre stands out as fundamental because it is involved in all other defensive operations carried on by the mind within itself. It will be noticed that I speak of 'defensive manoeuvres and operations', and not, as in the classic Freudian terminology, of 'defence mechanisms'. 'Mechanism' is a bad term because it is an impersonal term and implies a mechanistic theory of mental life. What we are really dealing with is not impersonal psychic processes but a person feeling driven to defend himself against other persons because he experiences them as hostile and frustrating. He reacts with an impulse of *aggressive rejection*. He wants to drive off, or annihilate, or in any way get rid of the 'bad objects' who thwart, frighten or anger him, and who fail to meet his personal needs. He may not be able to get rid of them in outer reality but he carries on the war against them inside his own mind. He acquires a mental image or replica of the bad object and then feels aggressively rejective against that. Now he is in a position, at least partially, to drive it away and get rid of it. He can, at any rate, drive it out of his conscious waking mind, forget it, bury it in oblivion and in some deeper unconscious region of his inner life. This is the now famous process of *repression*, the fundamental defensive operation against anxiety-burdened relationships with bad objects inside the mind itself. It is Fairbairn who has pointed out that repression is the internal counterpart of our aggression against external bad objects and that aggression is the dynamic of repression as a mental operation.

We must now note that it is repression that brings about the consolidation of the dangerous 'splitting' manoeuvres that form the second basic defensive operation of the psyche. We have already dealt, in Part I, with the primary tendency to 'get rid of the bad and retain the good' in our experience of significant people throughout life. In infancy and early childhood this results as we have seen in an actual splitting of the unity of the object within our minds. One of my patients said: 'I keep getting two different pictures of mother: in one, she is always dressed in all white, and in the other, in all black;' the good and the bad mother. At the beginning of his analysis this patient had an idealized conscious picture of his mother and had forgotten all about other aspects of her factually depressed personality that had disturbed him greatly as a child. Gradually in his dreams and phantasies there emerged this image of the 'black mother' as his repression on it weakened.

We have also seen that while the child mentally splits his objects into two, good and bad, he remains in fact very much emotionally tied to both sides of them. By splitting his object he splits the unity of his own ego: in terms of the patient quoted, one self clings desperately to the good white mother, and another self remains tied to, and feels in the power of, the bad black mother. By rejecting and repressing the black mother into his unconscious, he drives into unconsciousness a part of his own self or ego which is split off and disowned. *By the fact of repression this serious 'splitting' or loss of unity of the personality becomes a permanent feature of the organization of the personality*. In fact the overcoming of this splitting is the hardest of all tasks for psychotherapy and is certainly never accomplished completely.

We may say then that the basic methods of internal psychic self-defence, aimed always at getting rid of bad objects so that we ourselves may cease to be troubled by bad emotions and impulses, are *repression*, *splitting*, *introjection* and *projection*.

Introjection and projection are involved in repression and splitting. The external bad object is internalized mentally or introjected in an attempt aggressively to banish or master it. This, however, results in the creation of hostile figures inside the personality and sets up the opposite tendency, to ease the inner mental situation, by once more projecting the bad figures back into the outer world, fastening them on to whomsoever is conveniently presented for that purpose. *While repression and splitting are steadily maintained, there is a constant oscillation between introjection and projection, leading us to suffer under bad objects alternately in our inner and outer worlds.* Certain types of patient will alternate between periods when they are full of painful physical symptoms and feel attacked inside their body and mind, and other periods when all these internal disturbances disappear dramatically but they feel that everyone round about them is hostile, critical, trying to do them down, and they are dominated by a suspicious attitude to their environment.

Arising out of these basic defensive operations within the mind, there are many elaborations and defensive strategies of a secondary nature. The basic defensive operations are universal and common to all types of mind. The ways in which they are elaborated and applied during the course of development differ from time to time in the same individual, and differ from one individual to another. Innate 'temperamental' factors may underlie these differences, but whether that be the case or not, *individual differences in the operation and management of defensive techniques play an enormous part in the development and consolidation of overtly different 'types' of personality.*

If we think for the moment of the anxieties felt about the outbreak of dangerously anti-social impulses on to external objects, it is clear that these fall into two groups, libidinal and aggressive. First there are the starved, intensified, greedily devouring libidinal or love needs. The deeper the psychic level from which these come, i.e. the more infantile they are, the more likely they are to take the form of compulsive sexual desires or needs for bodily contacts and satisfactions.

The infant's life is primarily bodily. Personality values develop later. As one patient put it 'only bodily things feel real to me, a comfortable bed, nice food and the contact of warm flesh'. These imperious needs for security-giving bodily contacts, or for the bodily possession of the person needed for security reasons, are at bottom, to use the important Freudian terminology, oral rather than truly genital. In neurosis genital impulses turn out to be not truly mature and adult, but disguised forms of oral needs. Deep in the unconscious, sexual need is felt as a desire to suck, to suck in, to eat, swallow, devour and incorporate the object. This greedy devouring form of libidinal need is felt to be a dangerous impulse which leads to the draining, exhausting and destroying of the love-object. It betrays the individual into exorbitantly demanding and possessive attitudes. One patient reported that she woke up in the night terrified and feeling that she was nothing but one big hungry mouth. She phantasied standing with a vacuum cleaner (i.e. her own empty, needy self) sucking into it everyone who came near. Another patient, speaking of his jealous inability to share his wife in any way, even with her own parents, said: 'I need her, I want to monopolize her, I can't stand her taking notice of anyone else, I want her to shower every bit of her attention on me.' There is no doubt that *this hungry, greedy, swallowing up attitude to other people leads to the most acute anxieties concerning their safety. It is the fundamental psychic problem, the gravest anxiety experienced in outer object-relationships.* This fear of wearing out and exhausting love-objects (and, in unconscious phantasy and dream, of actually ravenously tearing the breast to pieces and eating and destroying it) is counteracted internally by repression, and externally by *withdrawal* from all intimate personal relationships on an emotional level. This was simply expressed by one patient who said: 'I'm afraid I can't make moderate demands on people, so I don't make any at all.'

This leads to the development of the *schizoid* type of personality. The work of Freud and Melanie Klein and of psychoanalysis in general until recently, centred mainly on the study of depression and the problem of ambivalence or the conflict of love and hate. Melanie Klein has recently acknowledged the importance of Fairbairn's work in bringing the problems of the schizoid personality to the fore. These he regards as of earlier origin and having therefore deeper roots in the unconscious than depression. In fact he regards the schizoid problem as the ultimate problem, underlying every other conflict, and he regards *the schizoid state and depression as constituting the two fundamental psychic dangers. They function as defences against the dangers of anti-social outbreaks, but in themselves they represent the ultimate and irreducible ways in which a human being can become psychically crippled and devitalized.*

I have elsewhere described these two problems as follows:

'The nature of the two ultimately dangerous situations may be simply described. When you want love from a person who will not give it and so becomes a bad object to you, you can react in either or both of two ways. You may become angry and enraged at the frustration and want to make an aggressive attack on the bad object to force it to become good and stop frustrating you; like a small child who cannot get what he wants from the mother and who flies into a temper-tantrum and hammers on her with his little fists. This is the problem of *hate or love made angry.* It is an attack on a hostile, rejecting, actively refusing bad-object. It leads to *depression* for it rouses the fear that one's hate will destroy the very person one needs and loves.'
(H. Guntrip, 'A Study of Fairbairn's Theory of Schizoid Reactions', *Brit. Journal of Medical Psychology*, Vol. XXV, Pts. 2 and 3, 1952, p. 90.)

Depression arises as a result of the repression of hate, and the turning inwards against oneself, at the dictate of guilt feelings, of the aggression that otherwise would be directed openly against the external object. Depression involves guilty self-punishment and the hating of oneself in order to protect the needed love-object. It involves a large measure of identification of oneself with the object of one's aggression and is an

attack on the object in oneself as well as an attack on oneself.
It involves therefore an indirect expression of hate against the
object for there is a secret wish that one's own suffering should
hit and hurt those who cause frustration. In the extreme case,
the depressed person's act of suicide is aimed against those he
hates and implies 'Look what you've driven me to. Now you'll
feel guilty, and suffer for what you did to me'.

> 'But there is an earlier and more basic reaction. When
> you cannot get what you want from the person you need,
> instead of getting angry you may simply go on getting
> more and more hungry, and full of a sense of painful
> craving, and a longing to get total and complete possession
> of your love object so that you cannot be left to starve.
> *Love made hungry* is the *schizoid* problem, and it rouses the
> terrible fear that one's love has become so devouring and
> incorporative that love itself has become destructive.
> Depression is the fear of loving lest one's hate should
> destroy. Schizoid aloofness is the fear of loving lest one's
> love should destroy, which is far worse.
>
> This difference of the two attitudes goes along with a
> difference in the appearance, so to speak, of the object.
> *The schizoid* sees the object as a desirable deserter, or as
> Fairbairn calls it, an *exciting needed object* whom he must go
> after hungrily but then draw back from lest he should devour
> and destroy it in his desperately intense need to get total
> possession of it. *The depressive* sees the object as a hateful
> denier, or in Fairbairn's term, a *rejecting object* to be destroyed
> out of the way to make room for a good-object. . . . The
> schizoid is hungry for a desirable deserter, the depressive is
> murderous against a hateful robber. . . . The depressive
> position is later and more developed than the schizoid, for
> it is ambivalent.' (op. cit. p. 90.)

We mentioned that the anti-social impulses that are liable to
break out from the inner world fell into two groups. The
first was the intensely hungry libidinal need of the schizoid.
The second is the angry aggressions of the depressed person.

One may suffer from both kinds of difficulty and oscillate between them: or one type of problem may predominate and give rise to the two markedly different schizoid and depressed personality types. They account for the distinction drawn by Jung between the introvert and the extrovert, for the withdrawn and aloof schizoid person is the introvert *par excellence*.

As we have said, *schizoid apathy* and *melancholic depression* are to be regarded as defences only from the external point of view. They arise as a result of blocking the anti-social outbreak of hungry greed and angry destructiveness respectively. Viewed internally they represent, not endopsychic defences against internal dangers, but the internal dangers themselves against which endopsychic defences are needed. They represent the crippling and ultimately dangerous states of mind which the ego can experience in the two ultimate and irreducible types of bad-object relationship, the tie to an exciting but unsatisfying object and the tie to an angry and persecuting object. It is important to grasp the fact that it is the struggle, at a time when repression is failing, to prevent the return of internal bad objects to consciousness and their automatic projection on to external objects, and hence the struggle to prevent greedy and aggressive impulses from breaking out on external objects in every day life, that leads to the development of schizoid and depressive states in the conscious mind.

We may say that *there are three main personality types*, the *schizoid, the depressed and the mature*. In so far as we fail to achieve or fall short of maturity, we shall be found in varying degrees to have schizoid or depressed characteristics. It is possible for depression to overlay the schizoid position and some people oscillate between schizoid and depressive phases when they are very unstable. The two psychic conditions form the psychological basis and character of the two fundamental psychoses, schizophrenia and manic-depressive insanity. Depression is peculiarly liable to give rise to a violent pendulum-swing of mood in which the unhappy melancholic suddenly 'pulls out' of depression by becoming excited, elated and hyper-active. This attempt to deny depression ends with a relapse back into it again. (The third psychosis, the paranoid, will be mentioned later.)

But these two states of mind are only seen at their worst in these two psychotic conditions. Their basic characteristics can be seen in milder forms, and in varying degrees, at every developmental level on the way up to maturity. The psycho-neuroses are attempts as we shall see in the next chapter to prevent the development of a schizoid or depressed state in consciousness. Further, *since human personality can be stably organized short of full maturity, we find many very stable persons, who nevertheless manifest recognizable schizoid or depressive characteristics.* Though there is nearly always some overlapping and intermixing of the two different sets of characteristics, yet it not seldom happens that in particular persons, one or other will predominate so markedly as to give rise to a fairly well-marked character type. Any particular individual may fall anywhere along one of the lines in a triangular scale.

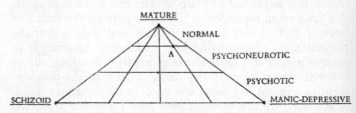

This diagram has no quantitative implications. It does *not* mean that the psychotic are the largest and the normal the smallest group. Psychotics are about a constant 5 per cent of population.

Thus an individual falling at the point 'A' on the scale would be rather more inclined to manic-depressive swings of mood (between cheerfulness and sadness) than to moods of unemotional aloofness, but well on the way to growing out of the internally fomented hates and greeds that cause these moods, toward a mature personality. The mature person is not afraid to have needs and seek their satisfaction but is not hungry and demanding; he can feel angry at frustration but is not compulsively and persistently aggressive. He can withdraw into the privacy of his own mind without being compulsively detached, and he can enjoy human society without craving for it as a distraction from inner unhappiness, or without upsetting all his personal relations by over-demanding or aggressive reactions. He can balance introversion and extroversion. Clearly none of us have arrived at the apex of the pyramidal scale, at full and complete maturity. All human beings show schizoid or manic-depressive tendencies in lesser or greater degree.

It is necessary, therefore, to describe briefly the main characteristics of these two fundamental immature trends, which are signs of the unconscious persistence of ties to internalized parental bad objects. We can best describe these as they appear in fairly well marked but stable types.

The schizoid person has, very early in life, encountered love-starvation. His personal needs have been repeatedly excited without being satisfied and he came to react to this intolerable state of affairs by getting, firstly, more and more hungry and needy, and developing a greedy, demanding, devouring attitude to all love-objects. Then he became afraid because his love, or need for love, had grown so exorbitant as to seem, and even be, destructive. *He became afraid to need and love, and withdrew mentally into a state of not having any needs and feelings.* In course of time a definite character developed marked by detachment, aloofness and coldness.

If he is stable, the schizoid person may be unnaturally calm in a crisis because his emotional life is all repressed. His emotional independence is, though only on the conscious surface of his personality, very marked. He keeps everyone at arm's length. You cannot get near him, or get to know him. He keeps himself to himself, mentally and spiritually, even when he is mixing with people. He is a 'dark horse', an obvious introvert. In order not to experience anxiety and conflict in human relationships, owing to his deeply felt neediness, he cuts himself off from emotional rapport and becomes an unfeeling machine for performing duties and activities in an impersonal, robot-like way. Since he does not consciously feel anything much, he cannot consciously feel anxious. He is unapproachable, and never lights up or enthuses. His praise is confined to saying that a thing is 'not bad'. He is often very efficient because not disturbed by feelings, and he is very often highly intellectual with an attitude of 'scientific detachment' to life.

The schizoid intellectual is very commonly drawn to scientific pursuits. A depersonalized universe that only has to be analysed and understood, not loved or feared or hated, suits him perfectly. Science offers him an escape from disturbing problems of personal relationship. Not all scientists of course are schizoid types, but very many are, which accounts for the hostile inability of many scientists to understand religion, for religion is pre-eminently about personal and emotional needs and relationships.

The schizoid personality in politics is one of our greatest menaces. Because he is so deficient in conscious human feeling, and is also unconsciously so hungry and devouring, he is ruthless, cruel, destructive, greedy for power and a swallower-up of human rights, a Himmler, and all in a calm, cold, calculating way.

The schizoid person may cover over his lack of genuine feeling with the superficial mask of a sociable manner but his emotional responses are shallow. Often such people do not realize that they are not genuinely interested in anybody, or in anything they do. Their automatic aim is not to allow anything to stimulate or excite them. One schizoid young man said: 'My school mates used to say I expressed the most intense emotion by a faint flicker of the eyelid, I was proud of being so unmoved.' But he did not realize that this meant being inhuman, and also that, under the schizoid surface, fearful conflicts raged.

If the schizoid personality begins to break down, it is usually into apathy, loss of interest, and a sense of futility, unreality and pointlessness in life. He may commit suicide with a calculated bored attitude of 'there's no point in going on living'. His needy libidinal ego is utterly crushed and imprisoned within, and all human warmth has gone. Even at his best he is valuable as a machine is valuable. If he is religious, his religion is an intellectual affair, a philosophy of life, not a passionate, loving devotion. Schizoid persons are impervious to emotional appeals and do not 'get converted' in revival services, an experience reserved for the manic depressive type. The schizoid is the complete introvert.

The depressive person is opposite in all respects. He may very likely have been fortunate in his earliest experiences, having been satisfactorily breast-fed in an emotional as well as a nutritional sense. Thus the foundations are laid for a capacity to love. It was frustration at a somewhat later age, when his self-assertive capacities were growing with his general 'ego-development', that he reacted to with great energy, and so he feels more and more specifically the emotion of anger and the reaction of frustration-rage. There are parents who can tolerate babies until they grow into vigorous assertive little individuals and then they become hostile and angrily disciplinarian. Perhaps he was too suddenly weaned, or with the cutting of his milk teeth his playful biting at the breast was not understood and was too intolerantly dealt with by the mother. Whereas the schizoid person's strongest and most primitive impulse is to suck, the depressed person's is to bite. Very likely he actually did bite his mother and later his playmates as a child. As an adult he bites pencil ends, bites and crushes sweets, and socially falls into 'biting' sarcasm, or irritably 'snaps someone's head off' as we very revealingly say. Probably also he was too harshly and rigidly treated, and too early over-disciplined, in the cleanliness training period. He learned to love and then became provoked to anger and hate.

He is ambivalent and suffers chronic conflicts of love and hate towards the same person, at bottom his mother. His tragedy is that however well he loves, he reacts compulsively with sudden and even violent anger at the least frustration of his needs by the object of his affections. This has made him so anxious and guilty, so afraid of harming the very people he loves and needs most, that he turns his anger inwards against himself. He identifies himself with his love-object and thereby unconsciously both preserves and attacks that love-object in himself. The schizoid type of introversion is illustrated by thumb-sucking. He has given up external love-objects in despair of getting a response and seeks to be self-sufficient. This is illustrated by the dream of a deeply schizoid patient that she was longing for her mother, heard her at the door and rushed to open it, but her mother walked past her and ignored her. In adult life this patient refused to make friends. She said: 'If I begin to like people I soon begin to want them so much to like me and I daren't risk that because I know that sooner or later I shall find that they are not really interested in me.' So she remained emotionally shut up in herself. The depressive type of turning inwards is seen not in thumb-sucking but in nail-biting, in the person who hits himself when he is angry or knocks his head against something hard as a depressed child will do. One patient put this perfectly when she said: 'If anyone makes me feel angry, I feel someone has got to be hit and it had better be me,' so she would shut herself in her bedroom and punch her own body.

This depressive self-attack is, however, more usually observable in the moral form of self-blame, self-criticism, and the arousal of persisting guilty feelings. At its most morbid extreme this becomes the conviction of having committed the unforgivable sin. The depressed person's suicide is not like the schizoid ending of a life that has lost contact with the outer world and become pointless, but an angry brooding self-punishment which is also indirectly aimed to punish the hated love-object. In the more normal and milder cases, the depressed person is rather gloomy, sad, pessimistic, over-conscientious, moody and irritable, but also very responsive to sympathy and kindness. He can get out of his moods by occasional temper-outbursts which, however, always make him feel guilty again and drive him back into a depressed frame of mind; but he has a greater capacity for loving than the schizoid person. He is afraid of damaging people by his hate, the schizoid fears hurting people by his need for love.

It will be seen, therefore, why we say that these two states of mind are only defences in the outer sense; they arise from successful efforts to prevent the outbreak of damaging greed and anger on to the external world. Internally they leave the sufferer a prey to the two fundamental forms of mental paralysis, the schizoid apathy, loss of interest, and isolation (schizoid means 'cut off') and the depressive melancholy and inward crushing down of vitality. Fairbairn holds that these are the two ultimate mental dangers arising out of bad-object relationships which have become built into the structure of the personality. They involve the unremitting generation of anxiety in the deep unconscious, and if the individual concerned breaks out of the inner paralysis then he at once suffers severe anxiety over the disturbance of his real-object relations in the outer world because of his extreme difficulty in controlling over-demanding and angry impulses. This involves the need for the elaboration of internal psychic defences against all this mental pain, which means defences against the hidden causes of it in the unconscious structure of the personality. Out of this need there arise the two great groups of defensive operations which make up psychoneurosis on the one hand and character-formation on the other.

This leads us to the subject of the next chapter, but before we leave the question of depression it will be as well to note that this concerns preachers very greatly. The depressed person is already secretly accusing himself, not for sins actually committed unless it be for his occasional temper-outbursts, but for sins committed in phantasy or that he is afraid he might commit unless he keeps himself constantly depressed. He makes his anxiety bearable by feeling that he deserves it. He is, therefore, an easy target for the condemnatory preacher who may foster depression by handling themes of sin, guilt, repentance and judgment without insight. In fact the preacher who is given to too much condemnatory preaching is most likely to be a depressed person himself, and is finding relief from constant internal self-attack by castigating other people's sins instead. The depressed person, when he 'takes up a cause' is liable to develop into a fanatical crusader. It is a great relief to a depressed person to find a socially approved occasion for being aggressive, which is usually possible if you fight on someone else's behalf. He does not stick up for himself very well, but he can battle fiercely over other people's wrongs. Not that that is itself a bad thing to do, but when it has its roots in depression, it too easily acquires a compulsive character which turns it into a fanaticism: and fanatics are not always the best advocates for the good causes they take up. They get things done by reason of their drive, but all too often spoil the atmosphere and adulterate the spirit of that to which they devote themselves.

CHAPTER VII

Defensive Techniques and the Main Character Types

WE have seen that mental pain is at bottom a persisting chronic state of anxiety compounded of the fears, anger and starved needs experienced in what the abstract, scientific, but cold technical term calls 'bad object relationships'. Science, in its effort to conceptualize knowledge and preserve its hard-won gains of understanding, must make use of clear, abstract, general ideas. This is no great disadvantage in physics and chemistry, but the closer we get to human experience the more danger there is of abstract ideas falsifying our understanding. It simplifies exposition to speak of good and bad object relationship. The reality we must keep in mind is that of a human being at successive stages of infancy, childhood, adolescence and adulthood, struggling with all the energy of his innate vitality to live: to live not merely in the sense of maintaining bare physical existence, but to live in the sense of developing and fulfilling himself as a proper person, realizing his potentialities and becoming what it is in him to be. This he cannot do as an isolated self-contained unit. From the start the satisfaction of his needs, the development of his gifts and powers, and his achievement of a sure sense of being a real person, are all bound up with his relationships with other people, and fundamentally with those few who are specially significant to him, forming the immediate family world to which he belongs.

If his relationships in the earliest and most impressionable years with the other members of the family, and above all the mother, are, as we say, 'good-object relationships', i.e. if he is taken seriously and valued and loved for his own sake, if his needs are met and the development of his own proper individuality is fostered, then he has the opportunity which is his birthright of becoming a well-developed, mature and stable person whose 'ego' does not break down under the strains of adult life. To whatever extent the formative relationships with family figures are 'bad-object relationships' in which he is not loved as a person in his own right, but is unwanted, neglected, depreciated, criticized, exploited, forced into more or less rigid conformities to other people's convenience and ideas, with little or no regard for his own proper nature and needs, he grows up full of fears, hates and starved needs, becomes divided within and against himself, is unable to achieve much solidity and unity as a personality and is in a state of constant, unremitting tension and anxiety.

His original bad-object world, as we have seen, enters into his mental constitution as an unconscious repressed inner world in which he can live only a precarious and menaced existence of unending struggle to maintain himself with some fluctuating sense of personal reality.

In the last chapter we considered the primary defences against deep internally aroused anxiety which consist of attempts to get rid of bad-objects and to escape from bad-object relationships. These measures have the effect of separating off that part of the total self which is disturbed by bad-object relations so that, it is hoped, what remains can preserve freedom from the past, and be at liberty as it were to start again with the present day life of the outer world and to build up in it something like a capable and effective personality. Most of us are able to do this to some extent but with varying degrees of success. This success is bought at a price. Much energy must be locked up and expended internally in maintaining psychic defences against the bad-object world in the unconscious. To that extent we come to the tasks of our everyday outer life with much less than our full resources of energy available. This has an obvious bearing on problems of fatigue, lack of energy and loss of interest. It is remarkable how quickly tiredness and lassitude vanish if angry temper suddenly flares up. Lack of energy may, of course, have specific organic causes but is just as often a symptom of psychic frustration.

Another part of the price to be paid lies in the fact that the nature of the unconscious bad-object situations which must be kept repressed, and the nature, therefore, of the defensive measures which must be adopted to enforce and maintain repression, very extensively influence the character of the conscious personality which it is possible to develop. This personality must be restricted and rigid in proportion as it must serve as a barrier against outbreaks from the unconscious. The idea that the character of the conscious and socially adapted personality is itself not only an adjustment to the demands of the outer world (as, e.g. in terms of the demands of law, morality and the ideals of religion) but also a defence against internal dangers threatening from the inner world of the unconscious, was first fully developed by Wilhelm Reich on the basis of Freud's theory of character-traits as reaction formations which over-compensate for repressed impulses of the opposite kind.

Character-formations vary according to the nature of inner problems and fall into a few fairly distinct tendencies which when they are found in relative isolation, constitute well-marked character-types. These are closely linked with clinically definable psychoneuroses, since a psychoneurosis arises when the menaced ego has to adopt drastic additional measures to prevent a threatened invasion of consciousness by internal bad-objects which are breaking loose from the unconscious. Fairbairn has shown that the psychoneuroses, hysteria, obsessional neurosis and phobias, together with paranoia (which in extreme form is a psychosis) are not *disease entities* originating at certain specific 'fixation-points' in infantile development: they are *defensive techniques* employed by the ego in its struggle to cope with internalized bad objects, and so to ward off depression or schizoid apathy.

A definite character-type is associated with each psychoneurosis, in spite of individual differences and variations in detail. They are built on either a schizoid or depressed basis.

The Hysteric is markedly dependent, longs above all to be loved, is demanding and possessive, feels helpless, and has what psychoanalysts call an 'oral character', i.e. strong needs to suck in, swallow, eat up and devour love-objects. The hysteric is most markedly schizoid at bottom. *The Paranoid* is suspicious and feels everyone is hostile to him and even plotting against him while he himself is all right. He sees enemies everywhere, and they justify his anger and aggression. The paranoid person is the one most likely to lose realistic contact with his outer world and become a victim of deluded and fantastic beliefs about people forming conspiracies against him. He is then liable to turn dangerous and even homicidal. But in milder forms the suspicious and rather paranoid character is familiar. According to Fairbairn the Hysteric looks for his good objects in his outer world and feels a prey to his bad objects inside. Hence he is an ill and suffering person always in dire need of sympathy, loving care, nursing and medical attention. The paranoid person is the opposite. He identifies himself with his good objects and preserves them in himself so that he feels he is all right, but he sees all his bad objects in his outer world so that he feels socially victimized rather than ill. He is reserved, keeps himself to himself, and he too is basically schizoid.

The Obsessional person has a passion for controlling himself and everybody else. His is a power technique and he strives for mastery in every sphere. *Control* is his ideal. In psychoanalytic terms his is an 'anal' character deriving from the period of cleanliness training. He is a great organizer and disciplinarian and is as strict with himself as with others. He is his own and everyone else's conscience, suffers much from guilt and is easily censorious to those around. Beneath his obsessional activity he is depressed. *The Phobic person* is the opposite of the obsessional. He does not seek to master and control but to evade and avoid. He keeps away from all situations which arouse anxiety in him and restricts himself to situations in which he feels safe. He is often agoraphobic and claustrophobic by turns, rushing into the small safe place

from the frightening large outer world, and then feeling shut
in and smothered and rushing out again only to face a renewal
of the former anxieties. The phobic person often oscillates
between depression and schizoid withdrawal. Fairbairn regards
the phobic person as trying to see and deal with all his problems outside himself in the spatial and concrete terms of
material reality, as if they were all problems of staying at home
with good supporting objects as against going out and meeting
bad ones: or else escaping from smothering bad objects at
home to be free outside. The phobic person does not see that
his problems are in himself. The Obsessional deals with all his
problems inside himself in terms of crushing down bad
impulses (i.e. really repressing the bad objects that arouse
them) and morally safeguarding good impulses (i.e. really
binding himself to good objects conceived solely in moral,
rather than in satisfying terms).

It will be seen that these are four alternative methods or
techniques for dealing with the mental situation when
repression begins to fail (either because of the increased pressure
of disturbing conditions in the outer world, or because of
some internal weakening). Internal bad objects either of a
sexually exciting but depriving and frustrating kind, or of an
actively persecuting and frightening kind, threaten to break
out from the unconscious, and so, in returning to consciousness, threaten to complicate and upset relationships with real
people in outer reality. Thus the resulting psychoneurosis,
whether the symptoms be of an hysteric, paranoid, obsessional or phobic type, is not the real trouble. The mental
illness is a defence against the real trouble which is thereby
kept hidden. Many emotionally disturbed and unstable people
oscillate between phases of employing all these four techniques
in turn, though usually any given person tends to have a
marked preference for one of them. He then predominantly
presents a picture of hysteric, paranoid, obsessional or phobic
illness. In more stable people where the primary defence of
repression is still working reasonably well, the predominant
picture is of a character-type, the dependent hysteric, the

suspicious paranoid, the masterful obsessional and the restricted phobic person.

Beneath all that, lies the fundamental problem of character-formation, the struggle to mature from the absolute dependence of infancy, characterized chiefly by neediness and the urge to 'get', to take in, to incorporate, and to arrive at the mature co-operative dependence of the well-developed adult with a capacity to 'give'. It is a transition from needing *to be loved* to an ability *to give love*.

Formidable as are the problems of anger, aggression and hate, the problems of unsatisfied need and hence frustrated development are more fundamental. Anger is a reaction to deprivation and frustration and is therefore a secondary phenomenon. If carried far enough, the analysis of depression, i.e. of guilt and aggression turned inwards, leads deeper down to the schizoid problem of unsatisfied and over-stimulated needs, of urgent, hungry demand, and of acute anxiety over the *devouring* and therefore unintentionally *destructive* quality of the need felt towards other people. Ethically, such a person is condemned as selfish, lacking in consideration for others, possessive and only concerned to get his own way and take care that he is provided for. Morally considered these are unlovely characteristics and the hungry schizoid person, already frightened lest his demandingness should wear out or drive away the very people for whom he feels such an acute want, is often very ready to accept the moral disapproval and turn it against himself in an additional effort to gain control of the dangerous forces within. What Fairbairn speaks of as 'the moral defence' and what Freud called the super-ego can be operated against both aggressive and hungry incorporating impulses. When the schizoid person does this he produces the classic schizoid state of detachment, mechanical activity and emotional apathy and begins to suffer from loss of interest and the feeling of futility about all he does.

What does this mean? It means in effect that he and his needs are considered not to be important, and he exists only to 'fit in' to other people while he goes hungry and unsatisfied.

The fiercely oral and incorporating quality of the neurotic need to be loved is not a natural survival of the normal infant's predominant need to 'get' and inability to 'give': it is a starved, frustrated, specially intense sense of need, and it has a certain quality of 'desperation' about it like the hunger of a man who might well die of starvation. While the needy schizoid is being condemned for being selfish, deep within himself he feels he is engaged in a desperate struggle to get possession of the very means of subsistence, and it is a life and death issue.

What, however, are those frustrated needs? They frequently emerge in frankly physical form as compulsive cravings for food, drink, sexual experiences, bodily contacts, cigarettes. Such cravings are largely symbolic substitutes, hysterical conversion phenomena in which a bodily need is substituted for what is really a personality need. The same sense of persistent craving may likewise attach to goods of chiefly mental import, such as books, gramophone records, social intercourse and the multiplication of friendships. The craving to amass more and more money links the two since money gives power to gratify all needs, both of the body and the mind.

Yet the striking thing is that however much the hungry schizoid person gets of what he wants, he is still never satisfied. The sense of unsatisfied hungry craving goes on and on. One such patient dreamed of having an enormous meal which went on and on for ever. Clearly there must be something about this that is more fundamental than the thwarting of this or that specific need. In the end such patients are all found expressing feelings of hollowness, emptiness, and unreality as 'persons', and there lies the deepest problem of all. They are struggling to incorporate other people or any symbolic substitute literally to have something inside them to feel real with, because they have never been able to grow any secure sense of having reality in themselves. They perpetually face the threat of the breakdown of such slender sense of their own reality as persons which they have managed to acquire at the conscious level because in their inner world they are surrounded by bad objects for whom they do not matter, hardly even exist as persons in their own right. When the child comes to feel that he is only loved for conforming, obeying, being polite and good and 'nice', that he is only loved so long as he is suppressing his own vital challenging individuality and letting himself be stamped with the pattern of other people's demands, he loses hold on himself as a real person. *Loss of the ego, of the substantial sense of selfhood and individual reality is the last and worst fate of the frustrated love-starved schizoid person.* Often the developing loss of the sense of inner reality as a person is heralded by a developing sense of the unreality of the outer world, and he loses his objects and himself together.

It is in order to stave off that last tragic psychic collapse, a disaster equivalent to a veritable spiritual death, that the schizoid person has to develop such imperative cravings to 'take in' and incorporate whatever he can. The development to a level of maturity at which he feels sufficiently real and substantial in himself as a person to be able to 'give out' to others, is the process that psychotherapy seeks to promote. We shall take up that problem in Part III. Meanwhile one further question calls to be considered in this section. The repressed greeds and aggressions of the anxious person are vital dynamic forces and they fill the whole body and mind with tension which demands some outlet by way of relief. Devices for tension-relieving are the third level of defensive operations against anxiety or mental pain which we shall consider.

CHAPTER VIII

Ways of Relieving Tension in the Personality

1. There is a type of defence against the danger of disintegrating anxiety attacks (or nervous breakdowns as they are popularly called) which lies midway between character-formation and neurotic illness: the defence by means of tension-relieving devices. If we may liken the accumulated depressive and schizoid anxieties experienced in the deep, unconscious, bad-object situations, to a secret hidden reservoir, a kind of underground spring of boiling water, we might then think of anxiety-attacks as sudden uprushes of dangerously heated emotion comparable to the eruptions of a geyser. *Repression* is an attempt to seal off the hidden reservoirs and prevent any outbreaks at all. *Stable character-formation* is a method of consolidating repression by erecting a powerful dam of character-traits which are diametrically opposed to the emotions and impulses which might erupt. (This refers to character in its aspect of defence against internal dangers. It has other aspects of adaptation to outer realities, though its two aspects may mingle and coalesce in subtle ways.) *The psychoses* represent a complete bursting of the dam as a result of which the fantastic life of the unconscious inner world floods up into consciousness and overwhelms objective and realistic perception, thought and feeling.

The psychoneuroses are methods of containing lesser but still formidable outbursts of anxiety (i.e. anxiety over the threatened irruption of internal bad-object situations into consciousness) by means of the production of symptoms. The symptom is an unrecognized symbolic expression of some internal conflict by means of which the actual inner situation is prevented from breaking into consciousness undisguised. Thus a patient who had often witnessed her father striking her mother, had herself experienced sexual sensations when he beat her on the bottom with a strap, and who naturally phantasied sexual relations between her parents as father assaulting mother, prevented all those active 'bad-object phantasies' (and repressed memories) from breaking out into consciousness with violently disruptive emotions, by producing a severe migraine headache. This felt like something hard hitting or boring inside her head and led her to say 'they're all quarrelling inside my head now and I can't stand it'. But the headache was more endurable to her, evidently, than being literally, mentally plunged back again in consciousness into the early terrifying scenes of parental quarrels. That would have exposed her once again to the full force of the fears and rages she experienced then.

Midway between the successful defence of repression consolidated by character-structure, and the gap-stopping symptom-formations of mental illness, we find attempts to deal with what we may call minor outbreaks, small trickles of tension and anxiety through defences that are cracked but not broken. *Tension-relieving activities* are attempts to drain off some rising pressure of anger, need and anxiety so as to prevent a major outbreak. We may group tension-relieving processes into those which provide a physiological discharge respectively for anger, need, and anxiety.

2. *The tensions of anger* are discharged in ways that are fairly open and obvious. Such habits as nail-biting, biting the ends of pencils, biting and crunching (and being incapable of sucking) hard sweets, are expressions of a reaction which originates in biting the breast. Compulsive cigarette smoking which a person is really unable to give up, no doubt, contains an element of anger-discharge since it is a systematic act of destruction. On a country walk the vicious kicking of stones and slashing at grasses and nettles with a stick is the action of a tense, irritated person who 'wants to have a go' at something.

Short of physical violence, anger is relieved by irritable

criticism, sarcastic comment ('biting' sarcasm), studied depreciation, and by swearing and actual temper outbursts. Much aggressive tension is relieved by entering into competitive activities in sport, business and politics. Tempers not seldom get frayed on the football field, and perhaps even more in spectators than players since the spectators cannot work off emotions in violent physical activity. Not all the anger vented in political arguments is an expression of pure objective dissatisfaction over genuine evils. One of the worst forms of anger-tension discharge is to be seen in the harsh exercise of petty authority, especially in the home.

3. It is, however, the problem of libidinal tension-relieving, or discharge of the tensions of *needs*, that takes us deepest into human problems. Fairbairn has used his view that libido is object-seeking and not pleasure seeking, and that tension is the tension of object-seeking needs, to reformulate the classic Freudian theory. The classic theory assumes a biological process of development through oral, anal and phallic phases to the phase of genital maturity. It lays down that this organic process determines the development of character up to a capacity for mature, i.e. genital, object-relationship. Fairbairn's view is the opposite of this, namely that character develops, on the basis of good-object relationships, from immature, infantile, 'getting' attitudes to mature, adult 'giving' attitudes, and this determines the manner in which the individual makes use of his organic oral, anal and genital functions. The individual's love life will function satisfactorily at a genital level because he is a mature person capable of unselfish giving, a true mutuality. His love life will function unsatisfactorily if he is immature and will tend to express itself in the so-called pregenital ways, in terms of greedy, grasping, incorporating oral drives, hostile, aggressive, power-seeking anal drives, and even in immature forms of genital activity which may relieve tensions but never attain genuine satisfactions.

This raises the fundamental issue for the understanding of both normal and neurotic behaviour. *There is an absolute difference between genuine satisfaction and the mere temporary relieving of tension as a substitute for satisfaction* which has become unobtainable. The baby finds true satisfaction in the mother's breast but when that satisfaction cannot be had, the tension of unsatisfied need mounts up inside to a painful degree. Of course, that tension would be relieved at once if it could attain genuine satisfaction but if it cannot then he must resort to some device for the mere temporary relief of tension in the absence of satisfaction: so he sucks his thumb. Thumb sucking is a device for the relief of the tension of object-seeking needs when no proper object-relationship can be achieved. Naturally even the mere relief of tension is pleasurable, just as prolonged unrelieved tension is painful. But it is an evanescent pleasure which is not associated with any permanent abiding satisfaction such as comes from a secure and genuine relationship with another person to whatever degree of completeness is appropriate to the individual's stage of development.

In infancy the undeveloped ego is almost solely a body-ego and cannot experience and enjoy relationship in any other terms than those of bodily excitement and contact. As the child develops it becomes increasingly capable of relationships which are less and less exclusively in terms of the body, and more and more a matter of richly meaningful relationships in terms of the total personality. Once we have left infancy behind and the ego has begun to attain an increasing degree of elaboration and development in the direction of adult maturity, relationships exclusively in terms of the body can never really meet our need and are never fully satisfying. Not that the body can be left out. We might put it this way that so long as a person has a body that body is the instrument of sensuous and active relationship with the material outer world, including other persons. But the body is more and more only an instrumental part of the whole of personality. The place of primary importance it holds in infancy comes to be taken by the total personality, and by personality characteristics such as interests and abilities, maturity of character and richness of spontaneous productive and creative capacity. The difference is striking if we compare a selfish nitwit who has an attractive body, and a truly valuable person with a body of no outstanding aesthetic charm. In infancy the need for object relations is a need for sensuously and emotionally satisfying bodily contacts. In adult life the importance of the body-factor does not disappear, though it certainly decreases in importance as one grows older. The adult need of object-relations is not primarily a need for body-relations but a need for a fully personal relationship, the significant characteristics of which are things like mutual understanding, appreciation and valuation of the other person intrinsically, the affirmation of him as valuable in himself, and delight in what is often called 'spiritual affinity', shared activities and interests, and spontaneous mutual communication and communion uninhibited by competitive and anxious feelings.

Freud, starting with the biological organism, concluded that the basic human motive is the desire for pleasure, by which he meant the pleasure of the relief of organic tension. Because of his tie to instinct theory he did not realize that in human psychology, 'personality' and 'personal relationships' are the real keys to all that happens. The mature adult human being does not seek organic pleasures primarily, but creative self-expression in the medium of fully personal relationships. Fairbairn has pointed out that explicit pleasure-seeking represents a deterioration of human behaviour consequent upon the failure to achieve good object-relations on a properly personal level (Psychoanalytic Studies of the Personality, p. 139).

What we are confronted with here, in the distinction between the pleasure-motive and the personal or object-relations motive, is the distinction we have already made between tension-relieving and true satisfaction. This runs back to basically different concepts of man, as organism and person. It is also the difference between mature object-relations on an adult level, and a falling back on immature object-relations on a childhood, bodily level because the developmental way forward seems barred. Large numbers of human beings live permanently much more on the level of tension-relieving activities which do not involve genuine human relationships and satisfactions than on the level of the real and permanent satisfactions of a fully personal life. The result of this inability to achieve properly personal relations is an ever-increasing sense of frustration and discontentment. People feel thwarted and as if they are always 'missing the real thing' for which one lives. We come here upon that 'basic need' which lies behind and causes Karen Horney's 'basic anxiety'. An intense but *repressed* hunger develops as we have seen, and is kept going by both external and internal frustration. Externally one may be tied to people and circumstances which do not offer much opportunity for good personal relationships; internally one may be much less capable of integrating relationships on a properly personal level than is apparent.

Serious inability to make satisfying human contacts in the 'here and now' results in a tense inner loneliness and sense of frustration, out of which inner tension steadily mounts as it is dammed up inside with no proper outlet. But the tension is a tension of *hungry need*. A vicious circle is created. Inability all through life to form good and mature personal relationships, whether on the level of business or professional comradeship, personal friendships, or marriage, will have resulted in the present day in an environmental situation which contains in actual fact but meagre possibilities of true satisfaction. Internal and external starvation, reinforce each other.

The result is invariably that *the individual is driven back on merely tension-relieving processes. 'Basic need', denied satisfaction on a mature personal level, has no option but to regress to the immature and exclusvely bodily level*. Needs are felt in the form of uncomfortable and even painful *bodily* tensions and disturbances and must be relieved as such.

There is a great variety of tension-relieving processes as substitutes for fully personal and satisfying relationships. We may divide these into two groups, pseudo-relationships and private activities. There are many activities which human beings engage in, in company with one another, which may, but do not necessarily, involve genuine personal relationship.

It is possible to do anything whatsoever with and for people without having any genuine *rapport* with them. These activities will have a really personal quality and be a medium of friend-ship for those who are capable of it, but are often embarked on as a substitute for it by people who cannot feel simply and positively towards their human kind. Many people plunge into restless and compulsive activity in athletics, social pleasure-seeking and indiscriminate sexual relationships to relieve the inner tensions of object-hunger which they cannot satisfy on personal levels. A sexual relationship which is a part of, and one way of expressing, a mature 'union of true minds', is one thing. Acts of sexual intimacy compulsively resorted to to relieve a deep nagging sense of isolation and frustration at personal levels are a quite different thing. Extra-marital inter-course is often regarded today as evidence of modern en-lightenment and freedom from narrow moral prejudices. In fact it is usually a mere tension-relieving process which con-tains very little in the way of fully personal love and valuation of the partner. The sex act according to Freud's theory is not a personal relationship but a tension-relieving process in which the sex-object is not a loved person with whom there is a profound sharing of life but a necessary means to the end of discharging organic tensions and obtaining the resulting pleasures. It is in such matters as this that Freud's biological theory has come to be so widely recognized as unsatisfactory. There is little doubt that sexual relations in many marriages are on the level of the baby's thumb-sucking, a substitute activity to relieve the tension of unsatisfied needs in the absence of a real relationship between husband and wife as persons. One of my patients was told openly by her husband that he only married her to have sexual satisfactions, and when their difficult relationship as persons interfered with her physical responsiveness he said she was no use to him.

The second group of tension-relieving activities are the private and solitary ones, of which the most conspicuous are phantasy and masturbation. These involve making secret and private arrangements to relieve the tensions of object-need without taking those needs to real objects. Masturbation illustrates conspicuously the relief of object-seeking tensions on a purely bodily level without the possession of any actual personal object-relationship, though it has the significance of internal object-relations in the unconscious.

The only alternative to these tension-relieving processes in the absence of effective therapy, is to become completely schizoid, to stifle all needs and eliminate all emotion and become a human robot for doing things without feeling. I think it must be said that *tension-relieving is better than this living death of the libidinal ego. It at least involves a refusal to surrender the need for personal satisfactions.* It is at least an effort to do something, even if it is not something adequate, to get needs met. So long as tensions need to be relieved the person is still emotionally alive. If a person gives up needs he has nothing left to live for, which is why the schizoid person so frequently succumbs to a sense of futility. But mere tension-relieving is inadequate. It is a letting off of steam which has to be endlessly and compulsively repeated because no permanent satisfactions are possessed. It functions like the spout of a boiling kettle which is actually a tension-reliever.

The seriousness of the problem only becomes clear when we look into the tragedy of the bankruptcy of personality involved, as with the patient who remarked: 'The only things that have any meaning for me are bodily things, lying warm in bed, eating sweets and nuts and cakes, being close to someone and feeling warm flesh. I don't seem able to find any interest in anything else.' In conformity with this complete inability to enter into relationships as a 'person', when she was alone and had no routine work to do and nobody to be 'grafted on to' (as she was in one of her dreams) she literally had a blank mind. She did not know what she wanted to do, she could not think of anything, in spite of being a normally capable and intelligent person. She had in fact no proper personality of her own and so was incapable of relating herself personally to anyone else. She had, as it were, nothing but a body to put in touch with another person.

One very schizoid patient could not talk because she seemed empty, so long as she sat opposite to me at some distance, and became able to talk if she sat in my chair with me sitting close by so that she could get hold of my hand when she felt unreal. She remarked: 'You can't possibly be really interested in me. I haven't got anything to give. There's nothing in me to mean anything to anyone.' The only thing that relationship could mean to her in her deeper feeling was a contact of bodies which had no personalities in them. Another patient got frightened on the couch and jumped up and came and sat in a chair close to me and said: 'Can I touch you, I can't feel that you're real.' Only a body to touch was real. Another woman patient had for years exploited her feminine charm to get lovers, yet hated sexual relations. It was the only way that seemed real to her of escaping isolation and getting into a relationship.

What is a personal relationship? It is a relationship between two people who have both matured sufficiently to be capable of independence in the sense of not becoming a prey to deep anxiety if they have to stand alone and rely on themselves. They will each have developed a definite and positive personality of their own, with the riches of stored experience and real interests. They have therefore something to give and are not in a chronic state of neediness with compulsive 'getting' cravings. They are able to appreciate each other's real and valuable qualities, and can both give and receive easily and without anxiety. They value each other intrinsically, and in this relationship they can both feel the security of being valued, accepted, and understood, and the satisfaction of each understanding and valuing the other for personal qualities of intrinsic worth. Their relationship will mutually enrich them and in it they will each retain the freedom and independence of their own integrity and worth as individuals. If they are a married couple their sexual relationship will be a spontaneous expression of their mutual desire for each other and their mutual self-giving in love.

Nothing approaching this fully mature capacity for personal

relationship is achieved by many people. No one achieves it completely. We can but approximate to it in greater or less degree. But in order to have any reasonable chance of developing this capacity for mature personal relationship, in which alone the tension of our basic, libidinal, object-seeking need can reach genuine satisfactions, it is essential that as a child one should have been able to experience real and good relationship with parents. We cannot become capable of entering into good human relations on mature adult levels of partnership in work, friendship and marriage, if our relations with parents in childhood were fraught with fear, distrust and resentment, and experienced in atmospheres of oppression, tension and quarrelling. One must experience good relationships early in order to gain experience of them and a capacity to enjoy them and contribute to them.

If bad relationships are experienced in childhood to any degree they are reproduced and perpetuated in the growing mind of the child and form an unconscious and infantile part of the structure of the personality as we have seen. Thereafter they tend to be lived out again and again automatically and blindly, in terms of the individual's contemporary outer life stage by stage. No security is felt within and no true and sufficient satisfactions of basic needs are experienced without. The individual can only fall back on the experiencing of persisting bodily and mental excitements and tensions which can only be temporarily and recurrently eased by the various tension-relieving processes. These will tend more and more to revert to the bodily level of the life of the child. The individual is driven back on infantile ways of wanting love-needs met, because the mature ways are not available. Since, once infancy is past, the child's libidinal strivings are allowed less and less open gratification on bodily levels, regressive libidinal tension-relieving comes to be carried on as a secret, private internal or underground activity to the accompaniment of ever renewed anxiety and guilt.

4. *Anxiety Tension-Relieving*. The relief of libidinal and aggressive tensions automatically relieves the tension of

anxiety felt concerning them, though it may create secondary social anxieties and guilt. Specific ways of relieving the tensions of anxiety are not so obvious as in the case of the discharge of libidinal and aggressive drives. The characteristic bodily accompaniments of anxiety such as palpitation, tremor, sweating and breathlessness, usually arouse further anxiety. Perhaps the most clear-cut tension-relieving device here is the substitution of a lesser for a greater worry. What the anxiety is really about remains hidden and unconscious, and a compulsive worrying habit fastens on one trivial thing after another. Then the unfortunate individual concerned is reduced to the commonly recognized state of 'having to have something to worry about'. Was the bath or gas tap turned off, or the electric fire switched off? Was the coal fire left safe or the door locked or the windows fastened? Has Johnny gone out warmly enough dressed or will he meet with an accident now he has a bicycle? If someone is not home at the time expected, a fever of anxiety is felt till he arrives. If a friend is a bit preoccupied that is an opportunity for worrying over whether he or she is losing interest, or offended or what not.

The possibilities of finding something to worry about are endless. If this grows too great it becomes a definite anxiety-hysteria, but in milder forms it acts as a device for relieving the tensions of anxiety while keeping the real source of the anxiety out of consciousness. If such a worrying person found no means of giving outward expression and vent to his anxiety, it would accumulate under repression and lead to more serious consequences such as a clinically definable psychoneurosis.

Part III.

MENTAL HEALING

CHAPTER IX

The Difficulty of Becoming a Real Person

IN Part I we studied the nature and origins of mental pain or
chronic anxiety and in Part II the natural and automatic
defences set up as part of the mental organization to master
or ward off mental pain. We have now to address ourselves to
the constructive and most difficult part of our enquiry, the
possibility and means of alleviating or eliminating mental
pain. Techniques of mental healing have flourished all down
the ages in primitive cults and in the great world religions.
With the development of science in the modern world, and
particularly with the turning of its searchlight of enquiry on
to human nature there has come about a great proliferation
of what purport to be scientific, psychological techniques of
mental healing. Psychotherapy was 'put on the map' in a big
way, first by the development of hypnosis from Mesmer,
Charcot, Janet and others, and then by the creation of the
broadly psychoanalytical approach by Freud, Jung and Adler.

It was inevitable that the religious and the scientific (medical)
methods of mental healing should find themselves face to face
with each other on the common ground of the mental suffering of human beings. Sometimes they have confronted each
other as hostile rivals each claiming a monopoly of the right
to try to relieve man's mental pain. At other times they have
found common viewpoints and enough humility to seek to
work together as partners. The arid Victorian conflict of
religion and science was not a good background for the study
of the mental or personal suffering of man, and it is a gain
that in its most sterile and dogmatic forms it is now out-
moded. It would seem likely that most of all in the field of

these problems religion and science will be compelled to seek a more profound mutual understanding.

To pave the way for this it may be observed that religion must learn to outgrow the credulous, blind and miracle-mongering enthusiasms of many so-called 'Faith-Healing' movements. Dr. Leslie Weatherhead in his book *Religion and Healing*, has done a signal service in subjecting the claims of such movements and techniques to a very frank and careful scrutiny, leading to the debunking of many claims to cures. Everyone interested seriously in this important matter should study carefully his chapters on Lourdes, Christian Science, Faith Healing Missions and the Laying on of Hands. Religious people must learn not to use 'Faith' as a cover for ignorance and for a fear of facing facts.

On the other hand the scientifically and medically minded must learn to recognize that 'man does not live by bread alone' and that he cannot be healed in mind by an approach that is concerned only with his body, or even with his psyche viewed in an impersonal way as an 'apparatus' (Freud) for adjusting a biological organism to its environment. The history of modern psychotherapy will probably in the end be most illuminated when it is seen as a struggle to free psychological science from the unrealistic limitations of deterministic, materialistic, and biological concepts of man as 'nothing but' an organism; and to achieve a psychodynamic understanding of man as a person, whose significant and real life is on what we may broadly call the spiritual plane of the achievement of personal reality and the sustaining of inter-personal relations.

With these two conditions fulfilled, psychological science and religion may, and indeed must, co-operate to determine how man's psychic and personal sufferings can be relieved. It is a veritable problem of 'the cure of souls', not only in the original and traditional meaning of 'cure' as 'care', but also in our present and more familiar usage of 'healing'.

In a paper on 'The Therapeutic Factor in Psychotherapy' (*Brit. J. of Med. Psychol.*, 1952, p. 116) I expressed the view

that religion is the historical form under which mankind
has striven to achieve mental healing. 'Religion has always
stood for the saving power of the good object relationship.
*Religion is distinguished from science as the historical form under
which the therapeutic factor for personality ills has been recognized
and cultivated.*'

Such matters as exorcism (or the casting out of devils),
conversion, sanctification, the forgiveness of sin and cleansing
of the human heart (or the overcoming of the 'bad' impulses
of human nature) and the attainment of peace of mind and the
love of God and neighbour, show how central the problems of
psychic conflict have always been to the religious interest.

In time past, if medicine could not discover an organic
cause for personality disturbance, then it was concluded that
the trouble must be one of demon-possession or moral
perversity or both. The sufferer from neurosis was handed
over to the priest in the witch-hunting middle ages, when one
of the stigmata of a witch was that typical hysteric symptom,
anaesthetic patches on the skin into which pins could be stuck
without causing pain. (This was a principal method of proving
whether a suspect were a witch or not.) If he was 'cared for'
medically it was by being subjected to such 'punishing'
tortures as being loaded with chains in foul prisons, beaten or
put through ordeals such as sudden ducking in water, to
compel him to return to his right mind and give up his
perversity.

Today neither the religious nor the medical mind would
subscribe to the diagnosis of 'moral fault' though that critical
and condemnatory form of diagnosis lingers in the impatient
advice still given, even by doctors, to the neurotic: 'pull
yourself together, you must cure yourself, I can't do any
more for you'. The futility of such an approach is reflected in
the complaint of one patient who said: 'My doctor says it
depends on me and I must cure myself, but he doesn't seem
to be able to tell me how; and anyway I've been trying to do
that for years and don't know what else to do.' This is matched
by the equally futile and naïve advice still given by many

representatives of religion that 'you must pray and trust in God, and if you had enough faith you would not need to go to a psychiatrist'.

These lingering remains of the older outlook in medicine and religion are, we hope, steadily dying out. Slowly, factual knowledge and general enlightenment battle their way forward against ignorance and prejudice, even in high places. There is still much fear and suspicion of the psychoanalytical approach in religious, medical, scientific and educational circles, and the blind spots in psychoanalytical theory hitherto must share equally in the responsibility for that. Yet, in spite of all, there is a solid and widespread acceptance of the fact that dogmatism and prejudice on either side will ill serve the cause of human betterment, and we must join hands and dig deep to find the truth that will set men free.

It is in that spirit that we have in Parts I and II sought to set forth what is now known about the nature, causes and natural defences against, mental pain. As we come now to consider its 'cure' we shall find ourselves compelled to take into account facts that would appear to belong more to the realm of religion than to science. It will be useful at this point to summarize the results of our enquiry hitherto in a form that will open up the nature of the problem of therapy or healing.

When a mother gives birth to her baby there comes into the world a nearly, if not entirely, helpless little organism which, however, has latent within it a potentiality for becoming something much more than the highest anaimal, for becoming in fact all that we mean by 'a person'. In fact the baby already is on its own simple level a person waiting to develop. Amongst its original capacities none are so important as the ability to cry and to suck; i.e. to express its distress when it experiences a state of unsatisfied need and unrelieved tension, and to accept vigorously the means of meeting its need when the mother's breast is presented. In other words the new-born baby is pre-eminently *active*, and what is more it is *spontaneously and uninhibitedly active*.

The baby as yet knows nothing of the systematized anxieties

and guilty feelings that will later develop as internal barriers
to the free exercise of its active nature and drive it into passive
developments. Its needs and its potencies, such as they are,
flow freely into its self-expression. On the whole most parents
are tolerant of, and solicitous for, the interesting, helpless
little thing for a time. What kind of adult person will it have
become twenty years later? Its chances of discovering and
developing all its valuable potentialities are not very great,
though they will be greater for some babies than for others.
The baby is born into a particular situation of climate and
race, nation and culture, economic and social status, which will
set limits to its chances for development as well as provide
opportunity and stimulus. What will shape its future even
more intimately is the fact that its mother and father are
human beings of probably very limited personality development and outlook. Their nearly automatic assumption will in
most cases be that the child will grow up to live much the
same kind of life and on much the same social and cultural
level as their own. The bare opportunity for many developments of personality that the baby could grow into will never
even arise. Certainly all of us have undiscovered powers for
doing things we shall never know we could have done, because the environment of our earliest years debarred us from
such achievements.

Is there not real frustration and consequent inhibition of the
active nature in this? On the whole the answer is probably
'No'. Where a child has undisputed gifts, amounting occasionally to genius, its powers show a remarkable facility for
bursting through the limits set by early lack of opportunity.
In any case, none of us could actually do *all* the things we are
potentially capable of doing. As we grow up we have to choose
among the many things that arouse our interest, and base our
lives on the selection of one interest that seems to us to become
paramount, while retaining several others for recreation and
as hobbies in our leisure hours (or moments). The adult does
not suffer from frustration of his personality on the ground of
some undeveloped powers, if the activities he does embark on

bring him reasonable security and satisfaction. Where there are gross misfits and distorted personalities, it is likely that the sources of frustration are of another and more subjective kind.

Let us return to the new-born babe and its parents. After the novelty of its arrival has begun to wear off, dangers to the baby's development of which it knows nothing, and about which it can do nothing, will begin to operate. Perhaps the mother has been ill or the father is worried about his job; maybe they did not really want a baby just at that time and its arrival aroused very mixed feelings masked by outward acceptance and conventionally expressed pleasure. It is amongst the commonest of occurrences for women to offer condolences to each other on account of 'another pregnancy.' 'Oh! poor dear, she didn't want another baby. She's got too much to do as it is.'

There may be much truth in that, especially where additional responsibilities for care or nursing of aged parents is devolving on the couple concerned, who may themselves have had to marry later than they wished. But over and above all such important facts there is the personality of the mother and father themselves. Their adjustment to each other may not be as good as could be wished. Their personal problems in themselves, with roots in their own childhood, may be quite marked. The neurotic factor in the personalities of parents is, in the end, the greatest menace to the baby. Mothers and fathers under analytic treatment often lament the fact that they repeatedly fail, in spite of their strenuous efforts, to avoid repeating on their children the palpable mistakes their own parents made with them. Temper outbursts, unnecessary prohibitions, too severe punishments, or an over-anxious fussing and an apprehensive approach to everything, may be among the parental reactions the baby has in store for it; and, more often than is admitted or even recognized, a fundamental emotional rejection of the child.

Another type of parent cannot tolerate the restriction on personal freedom that a baby imposes. The infant is weaned as soon as possible, and left to the care of older children or any (possibly unsuitable) baby-sitter who can be got while the parents go out to the pictures. When the baby cries too much every possible physical cause is looked for but it is not often asked: 'Is the baby going short of "mothering" in the emotional sense?' As the child grows up, the mother, busy all day, or the father, coming in tired from work, may push off the child with an impatient 'Run away and play, don't bother me now'. No one knows how deflated and devalued the child feels inside, and how its little heart sinks, and how in time it probably learns to cover over its hurt by a hard, naughty or defiant exterior, or else shrinks into itself like a snail into its shell from the outside world that seems to have little use for it and apparently regards it as a nuisance.

Parenthood is a heavy responsibility and it takes stable people to accept it with equanimity. While there are many people who possess a sufficient degree of emotional stability really to want children, and to be capable of loving them, yet the arresting figures for the incidence of neurosis throughout the community are also figures for the prevalence of incapacity for mature acceptance of parenthood. *In very many cases a baby grows up into a family environment that is subtly unsympathetic to its existence as an independent, vital, challenging little individual*: and nobody has the courage to admit the facts. Many, many unwanted babies are born into what are otherwise apparently good homes in a general sense. I doubt whether it is an over-estimate to say that 50 per cent of human beings are born as unwanted babies.

This basic, and usually unconscious, repressed, rejection of the child is very often over-compensated by too much meddling interference with the development of its own proper personality and interests; this under the guise of a care to see that the child is properly brought up. The result is a struggle to stamp upon the child what amounts to a conventional pattern in the parents' mind of what it ought to be. The motive, more often than not, is a care that neighbours and people in one's own social circle shall not criticize or disapprove of the child's behaviour, which would imply a criticism of the parents; 'I wouldn't allow a child of mine to behave like that'.

How often is the overriding motive a genuine loving care to foster the spontaneous development of the child's own God-given nature? More usually there is a wish on the parents' part to avoid anxiety and have as comfortable a life as possible by stamping on the child a pattern that conforms to their own familiar ideas. There are, naturally, all degrees of variation in this matter, but in proportion as there is a neurotic factor in the parents' personalities, so is it likely that the child is not loved for what it is and can become in itself, but rather loved in the inhibiting stifling form of approval for fitting in, conforming, obeying, not being rude or cheeky, not asking questions or answering back, i.e. for not having a mind of its own. One of my patients said: 'So far as my mother and father were concerned we didn't have thoughts and feelings. We were only there to do as we are told.'

It is one of Fairbairn's most important contributions, on the level of clinical observation, that he regards neurosis as caused at bottom by the failure of parents, and especially the mother, to enable the child to feel *loved as a person in its own right*.

The child, then, from earliest infancy onwards begins to experience 'bad-object aspects' of the mother and the father, and to introject these mentally and set up internalized bad-objects which are built into its very structural make-up in the ways we have traced in Part I. The child comes to live in its unconscious with bad-objects who exercise a perpetually disintegrating, demoralizing influence over it, as the bad-object aspect of the actual parents did in outer reality. Such a child feels always guilty, inferior, no good, inadequate, nervous and afraid, unable to cope, anxious. He has little self-respect and not much self confidence. A more happily loved child feels sure of himself, accepts himself and his own worth in a normal way, and feels to be a fairly solid, substantial little entity in a personal way, knowing fairly well what he wants, what he likes and enjoys, what he dislikes, what he loves and what he does not love in people as well as things, and is reasonably self-confident in his expression of his own personality. *The child who was not loved for his own sake and not treated as a person in his own right, never at bottom feels that he is one.* He grows up not knowing what he is or what he wants, unable to make up his own mind clearly about things and hardly having a mind of his own to make up. One such patient, a woman who had arrived in the forties, and was married with two children, still felt she was 'a shell of conformities to other people with no active "me" inside'. Such patients will often talk about feeling 'not a proper person', or hollow, empty, unreal, or feeling a vacuum inside.

Bad-object relationships in infancy and childhood prevent the child from developing a strong and consolidated 'ego-structure', a firm sense of definite selfhood with positive characteristics and creative powers. Instead of an inner sureness as being a properly self-possessed person with sufficient inner strength and resources to face and meet life with, *the individual whose early ego-development has been stunted feels unequal to every task and feels that he will 'go to pieces' under every pressure.* It must be understood that the 'internal bad-object situations' explained in Part I keep going this internal weakness of the essential self.

It is impossible for the individual to remedy this internal weakness by his own unaided efforts, so far as it is perpetuated in his unconscious by the repression of the earliest phases of his life-history, chiefly the experiences of the first five years. His conscious self has ceased long since to know anything about it directly. He only sees and is puzzled by its apparently inexplicable effects in the form of disturbing dreams, conscious nervous reactions, and/or physical symptoms of psycho-neurosis. He did, in the course of growing up, have to struggle from day to day to meet the demands of the outer world upon him, at home, at school and later on at work. He managed to a fair extent to do this by instituting, about the age of five or six years, a general and wholesale repression on all his experience in the first five years, which accounts for the paucity of our actual memories of that early time. It is active repression, not mere lapse of time, that has buried them beyond normal recall. We have forgotten and above all dread again to know anything about what insecure little beings we felt to be in those early formative years. That dread is the chief cause of the resistance to psychoanalytic attempts to bring it back to consciousness again.

It is as if a second start has gradually to be made in building up something like a stronger personality in terms of our later dealings mainly with the ever-widening world outside the family circle. The early anxieties and insecurities surge up again, though not exactly in their original form, in adolescence, which accounts in large part for that period being so much of a phase of 'storm and stress'. After that it is repressed almost if not quite irretrievably, unless it erupts volcanically in mental illness. Every effort goes into keeping the early insecure ego buried, and maintaining the later socially-adapted self firmly in the saddle in consciousness.

The later and ultimately grown-up self is, however, very much in the position of a house whose superstructure rests on inadequate foundations. Under stress, cracks begin to appear and anxiety begins to break through from the deep-down inner world. The 'strong man' in consciousness feels very much weaker inside than he appears to be outside. Thus one patient, a capable middle-aged professional man, says, 'I am looked up to and respected and regarded as efficient and competent, which I am, but no one knows of the vacuum I feel inside.' A middle-aged married woman and mother of a family says, 'I don't feel my age. Apparently I appear to be a mature woman and my friends seek my advice, but they don't know about my fears and how I have to screw myself up to do things.' Another quite capable woman says, 'If I am asked to do anything, I know I can do it, but my immediate feeling is "Oh! no I can't".'

It is only under deep psychoanalysis that one gets the opportunity of discovering how this deep-seated but much overlaid and disguised sense of inner weakness of the ego, the essential self, runs back and down to the insecure child of the early years buried deep in the unconscious. It is as if, where there ought to be a substantial, vital and active core to the adult personality, there is in fact a timid and apprehensive little being who feels that everyone else is bigger and more important than he is, that other people have little use for him, and who consequently has very little hold on his own reality as a person. The child in the unconscious can make as little headway towards security and self-possession in the face of his intimidating and devaluing internal bad-objects as he could in his actual historical childhood amidst adults who loved him for his own sake much less than they would have been prepared to admit.

At this point we come upon the *central problem for psychotherapy. We have to bring urgently needed help to this overwhelmed but fundamentally important part of the 'total self' so that he may gain a new chance to grow a genuine individual personality of his own and become a 'somebody' in his own right.* He must be saved, since he cannot save himself, from collapse into the abyss of nothingness that he feels and fears within. That would amount to the terrifying experience of 'loss of one's Self' and it is an experience by no means confined to those suffering from a specific schizoid illness.

In *Man's Search for Himself*, Dr. Rollo May, analysing our modern predicament, comes upon this same basic problem. In a section of the first chapter, headed 'The Hollow People', he says: 'It may sound surprising when I say ... that the chief problem of people in the middle decade of the twentieth century is *emptiness*. By that I mean not only that people do not know what they want; they often do not have any clear idea of what they feel. When they talk about lack of autonomy, or lament their inability to make decisions ... it soon becomes evident that their underlying problem is that they have no definite experience of their own desires or wants. Thus they feel swayed this way and that, with painful feelings of powerlessness, because they feel vacuous, empty' (p. 14). 'The experience of emptiness generally comes from people's feeling that they are *powerless* to do anything effective about their lives or the world they live in. Inner vacuousness is the long term, accumulated result of a person's particular conviction towards himself, namely his conviction that he cannot act as an entity in directing his own life, or change other people's attitudes towards him, or effectually influence the world around him. Thus he gets the deep sense of despair and futility, which so many people have in our day' (p. 24).

Dr. May traces this partly to broad cultural factors such as the lack of any secure 'faith', and partly to individual psychological factors such as failure to outgrow dependence on parents and especially to break free from the frustrating power of dominating parents. The analysis must, however, go deeper than that. The problem of 'dependence' is one that we must consider in the next chapter, but why, or perhaps rather under what conditions, does it prove so difficult to grow out of dependence on parents. We are faced with the arresting fact that usually *it is far harder to grow out of early dependence on a bad parent than on a good one*. The problem of the weakness, emptiness and unreality of the self is not the effect of a failure to outgrow early dependencies. It is rather true that *a failure to outgrow early dependencies is an effect of the non-development of substantial selfhood in the child as a result of family frustration*. It is precisely in bad parent-child relationships that the child's ego-development is weakest, making him unable to dare to break away.

Dr. May says very truly: 'the human being gets his original experiences of being a self out of his relatedness to other persons, and when he is alone, without other persons, he is afraid he will lose this experience of being a self' (p. 28). It is precisely when and because a child is denied the experience of being genuinely personally related to his parents, that he is unable to achieve the 'experience of being a self'. He then feels empty and unreal in a quite fundamental way underneath all his later experiences in life.

Such slender sense of reality as he does possess belongs to him only in the situation of remaining tied to the very people who frustrated his proper development. In the more obvious cases he grows up to be the child who never marries and never leaves home. More often he only manages to get away by substituting a new dependency for the old one and in order to get away from parents he marries a parent-substitute. But whatever he does in his outer world, the more hidden but ultimately decisive fact is that he is quite unable to outgrow an abject and helpless tie to parents mentally, and he perpetuates the early frustrating relationships deep within himself in his repressed unconscious. There he remains tied to the same bad-object aspects of parents that caused his early weakness in development. He lives on in his inner world in the original undermining situations and remains permanently weakened, yet afraid to break away lest he should lose what slender hold he has got on his own existence. As Dr. May says: 'Anxiety ... is the human being's basic *reaction to a danger to his existence*. ... Anxiety strikes at the very 'core' of ourselves: it is what we feel when our existence as selves is threatened' (p. 40). The persistence of deep-seated mental pain or neurotic anxiety shows that the individual feels, and is, all the time seriously menaced at the very centre of his psychic life, and has such a precarious hold on his own existence as a real self that he feels to be facing the imminent danger of 'loss of self' or annihilation of his sense of personal reality. He feels that at any moment he might 'go to pieces' as a personality.

This sets the task for psychotherapy. While often, for practical purposes, we may not be able to attempt much more than the relief of symptoms, or the *ad hoc* and superficial social or vocational adjustment of a patient, the real task of psychotherapy cannot be defined in any less thorough-going terms than the salvation of the patient's soul. He may even in some cases have to be supported while he is helped to discard a false, synthetic conscious self, and taken back to the beginning and enabled to discover and develop his own true self. Psychotherapy has only done its work in a radical way when the patient has become a genuine person in his own right. What he is seeking is nothing less than salvation.

CHAPTER X

Psychotherapy, The Cure of Anxiety

WE have arrived at a point now where it is clear that psychotherapy, to be effective, must be applied to the very foundations of the personality where the individual's hold on his own essential selfhood is always in imminent danger of being lost. We have already surveyed the main defences that are spontaneously erected within the psyche itself against the onset of this danger. These constitute, in their measure, blind attempts at self-cure, at safeguarding the conscious personality by blocking off the dangers invading from the world of the unconscious. But no real 'cure' can be achieved by the mere manipulation of psychic factors within the mind itself. Ultimately since the 'disease' arose out of *bad external* object-relationships the 'cure' must arise out of some new recreative experience of a *good external* object-relationship. This the sufferer spontaneously feels when he searches in real life for someone upon whom he can depend and with whom he can feel secure. This is admitted by the approaches of both religion and psychotherapy when they provide a God, a Saviour and a Church on the one hand to whom the anxious soul can fly for refuge and salvation; and on the other hand a psychotherapist who can go with the patient into the very heart of his problems and help him to win his way to freedom and a new inner security. In this chapter we shall deal with psychotherapy, in the next two with religion.

It is necessary to say at the outset that since all patients are not equally insecure and ill, not all patients need to be treated, even psychoanalytically, to the same depth. Patients who were emotionally disturbed but not so seriously disturbed in childhood, do not suffer the same extreme sense of persecution, depression and schizoid apathy, or the same absolute feeling of helplessness, nonentity and unreality in their deep unconscious, as is experienced by a person suffering from very severe hysteria and schizoid splitting of the personality. Patients who have had some reasonably good experiences in the past mixed in with disturbing bad ones, have something to build on. They do not experience the utter despair of the possibility of good relationships that paralyses the severely disturbed person. Yet they suffer a lesser degree of the same kind of problem. Any important degree of breakdown of good-object relationships between parent and child, results in a parallel thwarting of the development of sound strong selfhood in the child, and later an equivalent degree of incapacity for entering into good object-relationships in adult life.

The degree of psychic helplessness varies from patient to patient but is always present to some extent. We have to reckon with two different factors which may combine, or only one of which may be present in any degree from mild to severe, the factors of shock and of attrition. *Attrition* is the slow wearing down of the growing child's naturally spontaneous and active response to life, and the obstruction of its development in self-confidence and self-respect. This so often goes on all through childhood as an insidious process resulting from constant parental nagging, criticism, depreciation, disapproval, sarcasm, showing the child up in front of others, embarrassing him by talking critically to others about him in his presence; or by lack of interest in the child's own interests and activities, and lack of understanding of his needs for free self expression. In such atmospheres a child cannot grow any sure feeling of himself as a definite and worthwhile little person.

To this may be added the occurrence of *shock* such as a bad accident or illness, a sexual or other assault or interference, a too severe beating; or witnessing sexual or angry scenes between parents or frightening events anywhere. The child's mental organization is not yet very tough or developed to stand such things, and especially if the factor of attrition has already weakened him, he may feel overwhelmed and demoralized in a way that seriously damages his feeling of strength in himself; since shock peculiarly heightens the sense of helplessness and weakness.

This helplessness does not relate primarily to the capacity for repression, internal defence and the struggle to master anti-social trends. Patients on the whole are less helpless to carry out this negative task than to carry out the positive one of developing greater maturity and a more definite sense of personal reality and of power to sustain good love-relationships in present day life. Even the worst patients may show a surprising power of repressing the dangerous and disintegrating sense of unreality that affects them in their inner experience of themselves. They can go 'cold' and detached, aloof and unfeeling, and can carry on their lives in a mechanical way that precludes any arousal of emotion that would expose them to the dangers in their inner world. Yet though they are not helpless in this negative sense, *they are helpless in the positive sense, that if their deep down feeling of weakness and unreality as persons, carrying with it the sense of being quite cut off from real contacts with other persons, should break out into consciousness in full force, they cannot save themselves from it: they cannot become real persons, nor make effective rapport with other persons by their own unaided efforts.* At least that is true of the most severely undermined personalities, and even the less ill cannot find a true personality unaided but only force a synthetic one. The schizoid person, and the bad hysteric, and probably some patients whose extreme ego-weakness is masked by psychosomatic illness, genuinely need someone to make a move on their behalf, to take the initiative in rescuing them from their plight. They need someone to do something that is constructively understanding for them, so that they may have something to build on and to give them faith and hope. It must be remembered that the illness of the worst cases is due to the severest deprivation of constructive love in early life. *If deprivation of love is their trouble, then in some sense the supply of love is the means to their cure*. We have to determine in what sense it is possible now, in their adult life, to make good the lack of love that characterized their early childhood.

Some patients who, on the whole, were better loved in early years do not need so much to be done for them. On the basis of all that was good in their early experience they may comparatively quickly respond to genuine interest in them on the part of a psychotherapist. They may be able fairly soon to realize that his attitude to them is not critical, impatient, or depreciatory; that he does not 'blame them for faults' but really tries to 'understand their difficulties'. They may be able to grasp the fact that he has a tolerant and permissive, not a condemnatory, attitude to them. His tolerance is not a superior attitude to them as weak, nor an unprincipled attitude that might suggest that it does not matter what they feel (that would only weaken their realistic moral sense and make them more anxious by undermining their moral defences). It is a tolerance born of true human understanding and sympathy as of one who shares their human lot and knows how real their problems are, and has a proper respect for them as persons. The patient may then find it increasingly possible, as he lies on the couch or sits in the chair to relax and get over his anxious difficulties and talk increasingly freely and frankly. The analyst's experience and insight can be used reasonably quickly to help him to recognize what his real problems and conflicts are, how they began and how they have developed. The patient may be able, perhaps even without going too deeply into the unconscious, to regain a sense of hope, and of faith in himself and (via his experience of the analyst) in the possibility of meeting with genuine good will in other people. Stability can be recovered in a shorter or longer period which is, however, short of the very lengthy deep analysis needed by those who are more profoundly ill. It is with the less ill patients that a valuable pastoral psychotherapy can be exercised.

Every psychotherapist has experiences of securing reward-ing good results with the less ill patients in sometimes sur-prisingly short time. This will, however, not always be the case. All patients at times, and some patients systematically, delay progress in treatment by resistances arising out of their long previous struggle to master and discipline the weak child in them by their own efforts. They will say, 'I ought to be able to do this by my own effort or will power and not have to come to you.' They feel ashamed of having a weakened and undermined side to their personality, that shame being part of their struggle to suppress and be rid of it. They dread a type of treatment based on the uncovering and drawing back to consciousness of the timid child within, which they have fought so long and hard to subdue. They cannot feel sure that if it is brought back to full conscious awareness it can now be outgrown. They are anxious lest the hard won gains of their post-childhood years should be disintegrated and lost; lest they slip back into being what they once were without being able to climb out of it again. They take a long time to feel a sufficiently secure relationship with their psychotherapist to be confident about using it as a secure standing ground on which to solve radically now, problems they could not solve as children.

In the end treatment needs to last, if a radical and stable result is desired, as long as the patient needs for growing a full, firm confidence in the genuineness and reliability of the psychotherapist's interest in and respect for him as a person. The therapist cannot hasten that by professions and persuasions. The attempt to do so would only gloss over the difficulties that prevent the patient feeling it for himself.

It is, however, not only *resistance* that delays progress. In bad cases, the active libidinal ego is so crushed and immobilized by the anti-libidinal attack which is always going on against it in the deep unconscious, that the patient is actually *helpless* to make any move by himself. Sometimes a patient's silence is a phenomenon of resistance, of passive hostility and inward refusal to depend on the analyst for help, a kind of non-co-operation or sit-down strike. But there are times when the patient's silence is a genuine result of psychic helplessness. He cannot think, feel, or talk. He is unable to make any active response and is mentally paralysed. In that case treatment will become severely blocked if the analyst does not take it upon himself to make moves towards the patient, to take him by the hand as it were and pull him out of his frightened inability to move on his own initiative. The major problem is to discover what kind of help the patient wants and could respond to for it is very easy to 'put off' the frightened patient and add to his difficulties. There is no simple short cut to an answer.

I read recently a publisher's advertisement for a book by a specialist in short treatments. It read: 'The author . . . is a leading practitioner of the "short" or "brief" method of psychotherapeutic counselling. This is treatment which requires only two to ten sessions as opposed to much longer and more expensive treatments.'

That is what the public would like to believe is possible. Any thorough appreciation of the radical nature of the problems involved shows how superficial and illusory are such claims. For many patients, dependence on and needs towards the analyst are too great to admit of rapid recovery. Out of this 'treatment situation', as here described in general terms, four particular problems arise which we may call those of (a) dependence (b) transference (c) technique and (d) the therapeutic factor. We shall deal with these briefly in that order.

(a) *Dependence.* Well-meaning but really interfering relatives will often say to a person under psychotherapeutic treatment, 'You are getting too dependent on this man; it's time you stopped going', and will make the patient feel guilty about continuing treatment. Often the patient who retains some 'fighting spirit' and has kept up the moral defence of guilt and shame in a struggle to master this problem, will himself, as we have seen, exhibit a fear of becoming dependent on the psychotherapist. It is rarely recognized how deceptive this is.

It is, naturally, something of a blow to the ordinary attitude of self-respecting independence to come to feel markedly dependent on another person. It is assumed that the dependence on the psychotherapist which a patient develops is something that is created by the treatment itself. That, however, is not the case. Actually, the very nature of this kind of trouble involves, as a stubborn hard reality which cannot be 'wished away', the fact that the patient *is* a very dependent person. Over-dependence is part of his illness. He may have disguised it and refused to recognize it because other people are intolerant of it, but it is there, deep in him, and has been, all his life, before ever he goes to a psychotherapist.

The ultra-independent attitudes on which some people pride themselves, are a neurotic characteristic based on a refusal to admit an equal degree of dependence which is ruthlessly suppressed. It is interesting to notice how quickly the cry: 'You are getting too dependent' is raised when someone is under regular psychotherapeutic treatment, when the same cry is not raised if the sufferer goes regularly to a doctor for medicine. I had one patient whose husband and doctor voiced fears of her becoming over-dependent on me after she had been under psychoanalytic therapy for a year, while they ignored the fact that the doctor had been calling regularly to see her over a period of several years. The need for medical attention and medicines may very easily mask a deep problem of dependency. Many a man who would indignantly repudiate the suggestion that he has strong dependent needs, fails to recognize them in the fact that he grows irritable if deprived of cigarettes or cannot sleep if he is away from his wife. All the phenomena of marked conservatism and fear of change reveal the dependent trends of insecure persons.

The reason why the problem seems to be more acute in psychoanalytic treatment is that the patient's dependent needs are drawn out frankly and accepted with a view to giving the patient a chance, not to deny them and pretend they are not there, but to grow out of them; or at any rate to grow out of that part of them that constitutes a morbid over-dependency due to inner insecurity. The problem of over-dependent needs is in part due to a persistance, in the unconscious, of the anxious child's need of its parents, of the weakened ego that has hardly begun to feel able to rely on itself. In psychotherapy that is transferred on to the therapist who must accept it and become a substitute parent-figure if the patient is to have a chance to recover and grow mature. The patient depends frankly and with open eyes so far as he can, and works through with the therapist all that goes to make him feel so dependent, in order that he may outgrow it. If a good result is attained he ends by becoming a much more normally self-reliant person. He is then able to accept with much less anxiety and resistance the normal elements of dependence (otherwise so often felt as an irksome and restrictive tie) in all permanent real-life relationships such as marriage and parenthood.

In the severer cases the psychotherapist must be prepared to accept an extreme and even prolonged degree of dependence of the patient on himself, since here ego-development is most damaged. The patient may literally panic if he feels he is deserted and left to fend for himself. His sense of unreality in himself is so great that he literally feels he will collapse or 'fade out' if he has not got someone to hold on to, someone whose reality he can, as it were, borrow and absorb into himself to be real with. He must, and does, for the time being 'identify' himself with the person who is treating him. This explains what we have said about the patient needing someone to come to his aid and save him from his internal bad objects at first, before he can get a start in building up a personality of his own.

This, however, must not be dismissed as the problem of a few extreme hysteric and schizoid types. *The great majority of human beings have greater dependent needs, arising out of inner anxiety and insecurity, than they admit.* In settled times these needs are damped down by the support provided by home-life and stable social and economic conditions. They are to be seen breaking out in compulsive sexual needs, patent-medicine, alcohol and tobacco habits. They are masked behind aggressive behaviour and in recent years have erupted as a massive social phenomenon in the political need for dictators and authoritarian state régimes. It is the deep down need of the helpless person to be looked after. Yet, after all, this dependence is not at heart a bad thing. Those who cannot depend at all cannot love, and over-dependence has to be matured, not destroyed.

(b) *Transference*. We have already seen that the patient transfers on to the psychotherapist his persisting dependent needs for parents. That, however, does not exhaust the possibilities of transference, for the patient also quite blindly and automatically transfers the resentments, fears and hates he feels in his unconscious for bad parent figures. The two kinds of transference war together in his mind and there the tense drama of psychotherapy lies revealed.

It is only by working piecemeal through these conflicting reactions of 'love and hate', of dependence and resistance, to the analyst that the patient can at last rest securely on him and feel full confidence in him. Only then can he venture fully into his deepest unconscious where he is most insecure, to clear up its problems. It is a commonplace experience for people to feel objectively unjustified fears or dislikes of other people without ever knowing how and why they react in such odd ways. It is not realized that they are projecting into others the characteristics that belong to some important person in their past life who is stored up in their inner mental world. This phenomenon of transference is a part of everyday life.

It occurs however in the setting of psychotherapy in particularly intense forms. One of the things that condemns quick treatment to superficiality, except for those who are not very ill, is that it is necessary in them to prevent transference from developing. Thus an important means of clearing up many problems is lost. The patient is not aware of the extent to which he automatically expects from the analyst the same kind of treatment he received from parents, and sees in the analyst the same kind of personality he saw in parents. If a parent was aloof and cold he will begin to feel the analyst is aloof and cold. If his father was more interested in his personal pursuits than in his son, the patient will find himself thinking that his analyst is more interested in his psychoanalytical

science than in his patient. If the father was mainly dedicated
to money-making, the patient comes to feel his analyst is more
concerned to get fees than to understand and help those who
seek his aid. If the mother was critical and disapproving, the
patient finds himself getting nervous about speaking freely lest
the analyst should think badly of him. If the mother made
another child her favourite, the patient is troubled by the
feeling that the analyst is more interested in other patients than
in him. If parental silence meant unspoken condemnation,
then the patient grows uneasy about the careful and attentive
listening of the analyst to all he says, because he cannot help
wondering what the analyst is *really* thinking about him. The
possibilities of transference are endless and if they develop to
the full they become an intense sense of unsatisfied longing to
be loved by the analyst, and an equally marked hatred over
feeling frustrated by him.

In working slowly over all these transference problems the
patient is gradually clearing his mind of the many ways in
which the ingrown patterns of past relationships interfere
with his capacity for straightforward and objectively realistic
relationships with people in his present day world. Bit by bit,
as he comes to see the analyst as he really is in himself (not as a
perfect idealized figure who represents all that the patient
wanted his parents to be, but as the real human being that he
is), the patient is set free to see other people in a more real
way. As a part of that process he is all the time becoming
more real to himself, experiencing his own genuine perceptions, emotions and impulses and not those stamped on him
by his past.

One of the road blocks on the pathway to the therapeutic
goal, which arises out of transference phenomena, is the
patient's (unconscious) assumption that he must say what he
thinks the analyst wants him to say and will approve of. He
has grown up to trim his sails by the winds of parental
expectations and demands. He cannot, for a long time, feel
that he will now be valued not for conformity but for
spontaneity, for saying what *he* really thinks and feels, for

being himself. As he makes that discovery a growing liberation of his personality from shackling inhibitions takes place.
In this new, frank and openly realistic relationship he begins to
feel that it is safe and possible to become a person in his own
right, and to develop a personality of his own. Naturally all
authoritarian and disciplinarian ideas are death to his free
development of genuine personal reality in a relationship of
mutual respect and true helpfulness. Yet it is only in this way
that the weakened and demoralized child in the unconscious
(the inhibited and passive Libidinal Ego) can get a start in
growing up to self-respecting and self-confident maturity.

It is in the necessity for dealing with these transference
problems, and all the unconscious material they bring to light
that the importance of psychoanalytical knowledge, experience and technique is called for. Mere sympathetic and friendly
support, what we might call 'pastoral love and helpfulness'
(*agape*, not *eros*) is not enough. The analyst must be trained to
know what to expect and to recognize it through all its disguises when it comes. This leads to our third problem in
psychotherapy, the significance of the psychoanalytical
technique.

(*c*) *The Technique of Psychoanalysis.* It is recognized that as
time went on Freud became more pessimistic about the value
of psychoanalysis as an instrument of psychotherapy, and
more interested in it as a technical method of scientific
research into the dynamics of human nature. Today there is
an increasing tendency to distinguish between psychoanalysis and psychotherapy. It is dangerous to make simple
statements about Freud. So great was his insight and so many-
sided and large-minded was his genius as a pioneer investigator
into the human psyche, that almost anything said about him
could be disproved by quotations from his own writings. This
great man's work will be a seed-plot of ideas for a long time
to come.

Yet it is broadly true to say that while he began as a doctor,
and as a consultant neurologist, bent on finding out how to
cure his patients of their psychoneuroses, he was first and

foremost a scientist. I think the statement would not be disputed that the scientist predominated in Freud over the psychotherapist more and more. That must have much to do with his pessimism about psychotherapy and his enthusiasm for the psychoanalysis he had created coming to rest mainly on its value as an investigatory technique. *For if the illness we call a psychoneurosis is due at bottom to love-starvation, its cure is not likely to be achieved simply by a scientific analysis of its history and results.* That would merely represent diagnosis not treatment if it stood alone.

The range of Freud's genius and insight is nowhere more clearly seen than in the fact that he himself first provided so many of the fundamental observations necessary to develop psychoanalysis beyond his own narrowly biological formulations. He provided the material for a full-scale dynamic psychology of man as a person, though he himself never went beyond a psychology of man as an organism. He was a scientist, and science is not primarily interested in the individual *qua* individual, and moreover it depersonalizes its material when it studies human beings. Freud developed a theory of mind as a 'mental apparatus' for adjusting instinctual drives to the outer environment; the principle of mental functioning was the hedonistic one of avoiding pain and obtaining pleasure, the pleasure of the detensioning and relief of the strain of as yet undischarged instinctive impulses. In the last resort this detensioning was a physiological process on the analogy of the relief of sexual tensions by orgasm and detumescence.

In all this there is no conception of man as a person. One might hope this would emerge when Freud took up the question of ego-object relationships. It appears, however, that the ego is only a superficial phenomenon developed 'on the surface of the id' or instinctive unconscious. It is the aforesaid 'mental apparatus' taken along with the super-ego ('a differentiating grade within the ego', *Ego and Id*, p. 34) for regulating id-impulses. Objects are not persons having their own intrinsic value and loved or hated for their own quality: they are merely *means* to the subjective end of instinctive detensioning.

The whole process of character-development is made dependent on, and is merely a reflection of, the biological processes of the maturing of the sexual organs and instincts.

At best Freud's views turn out to be only a scientific version of the old traditional dualistic dogma of the soul as the field of battle between the lusts of the flesh and the moral and religious conscience: (i.e. the ego as the field of battle between id-impulses and super-ego). So far we have gained nothing but a highly abstract 'metapsychological theory' which casts no real light of understanding on the personal life of man.

Of course, Freud did not conduct sessions with patients in the language of this theory. There he helped the patient to reconstruct and emotionally relive his whole life history. In doing this Freud made discoveries and observations of truly revolutionary importance for the understanding of man. Unaided he laid the foundations for a truly scientific account of the process, phase by phase, of the psychic development of man from birth to maturity.

It is a tragedy that he did not realize himself that his startling discovery that conscience, or the super-ego, is an *internal psychic object*, a complex mentally internalized or reproduced parent figure, really invalidated his earlier id or instinct theory and opened up an entirely new explanatory principle. As we saw in Chapter IV, human life and the structure of the psychic personality could now be understood in a *personal* instead of in a merely *biological* way. Freud never lifted psychoanalysis to the level of a *personality-theory*. It remained what Dr. Marjorie Brierley calls 'a process theory' (*Trends in Psycho-Analysis*, p. 101). Though Freud did not talk 'metapsychology' to his patients, yet his theory dominated his therapeutic outlook. It was believed that the psycho-analytic technique of investigating the processes and 'mechanisms' of a patient's development brought about a curative change: as if the mere bringing of a repressed conflict to consciousness enabled the patient to solve it.

Freud in a way realized, when he seized on transference phenomena (another of his very great discoveries) as the most important aspect of psychoanalytical treatment, that the personal relationship of the patient and the psychotherapist was vital. But he regarded it as a medium of the technical investigation whereby past stages of the patient's development were brought to consciousness. It was held that the technique of psychoanalysis was the curative factor and the analyst was required to efface and depersonalize himself, to sit out of sight of the patient, to show no personal reactions and to function merely as a projection-screen for the patient's transference phantasies, and as an interpreting scientific intellect. It is little wonder that Freud grew pessimistic over the value of psychoanalysis as therapy, and that waves of therapeutic pessimism have recurred in the history of the psychoanalytical movement. It is now coming to be seen that *the technique of psychoanalysis is but a means of discovering what problems the patient has to solve, and his power to solve them is derived from the therapeutic personal relationship with the analyst.* In Fairbairn's terms the personal object-relationship is the important thing, in psychotherapy as in life itself.

This has been widely appreciated by American psychotherapists, particularly of the sociologically minded, 'culture-pattern' school (Horney, Fromm). Dr. H. S. Sullivan speaks of the psychotherapist as a 'participant observer' (*Conceptions of Modern Psychiatry*), a good term since it indicates that he is not just a detached scientific observer and interpreter but a person actually participating with the patient in the process of the cure. The psychotherapist cannot shelter behind a scientific anonymity and impersonality, or if he does his patient will remain unhelped and uncured. Psychotherapy is a joint enterprise of two people to solve the personal problems of one of them, in which, however, the other, *the psychotherapist, has got to take the risk of being a real person, with all his limitations as well as his skill and experience, to the patient, so that the patient may have a chance of becoming a real person with him.* He may not safeguard himself, and defend himself from the patient's impact on him, by mounting a pedestal of aloof superiority and authority. If he does he is quite likely to repeat on the patient the original injury done to him by an authoritarian parent. He has to be capable of being a human being without pretensions so that the patient may be able to discover what a genuine human relationship is. He will not shelter behind his technique but will use it tactfully and sympathetically, adjusting his interpretations to the patient's sensitivity and sore spots. Thus diagnosis and the discovery of the patient's unconscious problems develop slowly at such a rate as enables the patient to resolve his anxieties and develop his personality in touch with another real person.

This is a very exacting business and it both calls for and promotes maturity in the analyst. If the analyst were himself too immature as a person he would be betrayed into exploiting the patient in the interest of his own unsolved emotional problems. That is why it is an *absolute* requirement that the psychoanalyst should be himself first psychoanalysed, not merely to learn the technique but to increase his own maturity and fitness for the task.

The importance of recognizing that the therapeutic factor resides in the personal relationship, not in the scientific technique of investigation, is clear when we contemplate the wider bearings of the problem. Science, being morally neutral, can be used for both good and evil purposes. Atomic power can be used to destroy cities or to provide them with light and power. So a psychoanalytical investigation (like hypnosis, and also religion) could be used either to destroy or to develop personality. Religious influence has often been used to enslave the individual. Hypnosis has often been accused of being used for nefarious purposes. Psychoanalysis could undoubtedly be used (and totalitarian dictatorships may have recognized this as a method of softening up political prisoners) to reduce a person to infantile weakness and dependence so as to obtain a hold over him instead of to help him to regrow a truly adult self. It all depends on the aims of the person using the discoveries of science, a problem which in fact is a major problem in our world today. This leads us to the fourth problem in psychotherapy.

(d) *The Therapeutic Relationship.* Here again Freud saw further than his theory would take him. He stated in his essay on 'Analysis, Terminable and Interminable', that *the problem of psychotherapy is to bring adequate aid to the ego of the patient (Collected Papers,* Vol. V, p. 332). It is true that his theory limited him to the view that the patient's ego needed support against the innate strength of his anti-social instincts. In the light of our earlier exposition we can re-interpret this and say that what the patient needs support against is not the strength of his biological drives but the disintegrating and demoralizing influence of his internal bad objects, i.e. the legacy of all that thwarted his personality development in childhood. *He needs the analyst to be to him a mature parent figure in relationship with whom he can mature his own personality to the point where the internalized bad-object aspects of his parents no longer have power to harm and weaken him.*

We have seen that the process of psychotherapy or the healing of mental pain is one which is promoted by the personal influence of a dynamic human relationship making use of a scientific technique for exploring human personality. It makes possible a re-creation or re-growing of the whole personality by means of which the patient is saved from the crippling power of the living past within him. We must seek to characterize this human relationship between psychotherapist and patient more definitely.

In the course of exploring in detail in a psychoanalytical way all the particular and separate parts and aspects of the patient's total complex personality problem, *the analyst as therapist must provide for the patient both emotional protection and stimulus to mature development.* A dream of a married woman in the late thirties, a mother of two children, who had, however, been seriously mentally ill for a number of years, shows clearly the kind of need the patient feels. Just because her case was a very bad one it magnifies and clarifies the issues. Her childhood was marked by exceptionally ruthless rejection and deprivation of love at the hands of both parents, who also interfered openly and prohibitively in all the friendships in which she might have found some substitute for what she lacked at home. In her dreams she was a child again and the first two scenes were literal descriptions of what often actually happened between her and her parents. Her mother had been in a temper with her and she was following mother from room to room pleading to be forgiven and saying, 'Do you love me now, Mummy?' The mother merely ignored her and returned no answer. Then she and her mother were out shopping and the mother, still in an angry mood, was striding ahead leaving the bewildered and anxious child to keep up as best she could amid the crowds. She couldn't do it and soon realized her mother had disappeared, had deserted her, and she stood on the pavement lost and crying. Suddenly her father appeared and said, 'Stop this fuss, behave yourself and come with me.' She knew that that meant she had to walk quickly along at father's side without speaking, and as they proceeded she suddenly saw me on the other side of the road. She dashed across and caught hold of me while her father shouted angrily to her to come back; but while she held my hand she was not afraid and did not return to him.

At the time of this dream both parents had been dead for some time, yet here was this struggle going on in her mind in which she was trying to escape from them to me, and they were active inside her mind and pitted against me as the agent of her liberation. For some three years of psychoanalytical treatment she had been a cold, distant, mechanical being, often quite unable to talk, and when she did talk only taking part in the situation in an automatic way without any real feeling and without really entering into it. This rigidly impersonal mask, however, hid desperate needs and intense anxieties which only slowly and with utmost caution and hesitation did she reveal to me. She was for long convinced that no one could possibly ever be really interested in her, and if she let me see her real problems she would only meet with rebuff. So afraid was she that for a long time she could not even let me try to help her out in any way, but gradually the fact that I did not end her treatment as hopeless began to give her the first bit of hope and confidence in me. Little by little she began to move mentally away from her parents and their demoralizing and crushing impact on her ego and grasp at my help.

At this stage some of her worst anxieties began to emerge. Such slender reality as she did feel in herself was hers only as the target of her parents' anger and harsh criticism. Apart from that she was nothing 'in herself'. The mental effect of breaking away from them in her inner world before she felt she had a secure relationship with me, was to lay her open to attacks of depersonalization, and de-realization of her environment. She would suddenly feel quite unreal and lose the sense of my being real, and she was unable to carry on unless she sat in a chair close alongside mine so that she could touch me and so ward off the frightening attacks of 'fading out'. That, however, reassured her and she arrived at the point registered in her dream. From then onwards she began slowly to feel that she was changing and becoming a more human and friendly person, and a more affectionate person in her family life. One stage of her 'cure' was marked by her husband saying, 'You're not freezing me off so much nowadays.'

This case which, though a severe one, is not in any sense unique, illustrates the fact that the patient who uncovers deep levels of the unconscious first of all needs the analyst as a protector against emotional dangers. But for him the patient would succumb to intolerable anxiety, persecutory fears, and states of 'loss of self' or depersonalization. A vivid dream of a man of forty illustrates the position in a more symbolic way. He dreamed that he went in search of Christ, found Him and then went with him to a dark cave (the unconscious). At the entrance he became aware that a terrible ghost was inside and he fled in panic, but looking round he saw that Christ had not run away so he went back and they went in to face the ghost together. That dream, which points us forward to the chapter on psychotherapy and religion, was later followed by another in which he faced the ghost of his violent-tempered mother at the door of a room at home, while I stood by in the passage.

The patient clearly needs the psychotherapist for a long time as a protector against, or saviour from, the internal bad objects inhabiting his inner unconscious world, and as a safeguard against succumbing to the dreaded disintegrating states of mind they induce in him. That is the stage of maximum dependence of the patient on the psychoanalyst. A successful negotiation of the difficulties and dangers of that stage allow of the slow development of the second and more important aspect of the analyst-patient relationship. *Ultimately the patient needs the analyst to be a mature person with whom he can achieve a realistic relationship in which he himself is stimulated to the development of a mature personality of his own.*

At this point the fundamental nature of the analyst's relation to the patient becomes clear. *He must in effect be a stable parent-substitute with whom the child in the patient's unconscious can grow up to be a self-respecting and self-confident adult person.* All the emotional problems in the patient's relationship to his analyst, whether they be transference problems or realistic needs, arise out of the parental rôle in which the patient in his unconscious feeling automatically casts him. As he slowly works through and overcomes the projection of internalized bad aspects of parents, he becomes more and more capable of seeing and appreciating the analyst as a real person; and his realistic needs towards his analyst assume ever greater importance. The analyst must do something for him that his parents in some measure failed to do. This, of course, does not mean that the analyst must be, or try to appear, a superior or exceptional person. Any such rôle-playing on the analyst's part would be fatal to therapeutic progress. He must above all be a real person, not anxiously hiding his limitations, for it is precisely *reality in the realm of personality* that the patient needs to meet and experience in another person so that he can be real himself.

Slowly a sense of equality between analyst and patient will develop and this could only be retarded by a spurious familiarity. It must grow out of genuine experience. It helps the patient at this stage to realize that the analyst feels no need to pose as perfect, is aware of and accepts without fear his natural shortcomings both in gifts and experience, and regards himself as simply human, as one who has trodden much of the same path of conflict and anxiety as the patient, so that he understands the inwardness of the patient's suffering. In the early stages of treatment the patient often idealizes the analyst in such remarks as 'You can't know what I suffer, I can't imagine your ever having felt my weaknesses'. This should fade out into a realization of the analyst as an ordinary but reliable human being. If the analyst were not of 'the same flesh and blood' and 'of like passions' with the patient, the patient could only feel discouraged about overcoming his sense of inferiority. Idealization is a remnant of early attitudes to parents, to be grown out of.

But one thing that the patient must find in the analyst. He must ultimately become convinced that the analyst 'loves him as a person in his own right', that the analyst does feel a genuine interest, concern and goodwill for him for his (the patient's) own sake, and respect and takes him seriously. That above all, the spiritual love of *agape*, not *eros*, is what helps the patient to feel and accept and develop his own reality as a person and come to be a somebody in himself. This, naturally, includes the analyst's attitude of not trying to shape or mould or educate, not seeking to dictate any pattern or ideal (as parents so usually do) but rather fostering, and being genuinely interested in, the patient's discovery of his own distinct individuality and right to be different from others if that lies in his own proper nature.

CHAPTER XI

Psychotherapy and Values

OUR treatment of psychotherapy has brought us to the point
where our enquiry altogether over-leaps the boundaries of
psychoanalysis, at least as it was conceived by its creator
Sigmund Freud. We begin to find our theme leading out
towards the great ultimate problems, the worth of the individual soul, the question of values and the place of religion. It
is the consideration of the relationship between science and
religion that brings these problems to the forefront.

We have already seen that psychoanalysis, considered
purely as a scientific technique of investigation, could as well
be used destructively as constructively. At once the question
of the aims and the values of the psychoanalyst is raised. In
practice, of course, sound values are more often implicit
than consciously defined in our activities. Certainly psychoanalysts and psychotherapists as a group are as sound and
responsible in the exercise of their skill as any other group of
human beings trained to the direct service of their fellow men.
In fact, just as humanity has always expected of its religious
leaders a higher standard of integrity and unselfish devotion
than it expects of most other vocations, so the same high
demand must certainly be made on psychoanalysts and psychotherapists. It is an outstanding tribute to the sincerity and sense
of responsibility of psychoanalysts that they have made on
themselves the exceptionally exacting demand that they
should undergo a very long personal analysis before they
subject their patients to the process. Undoubtedly values of
the utmost importance are here implied.

The psychoanalyst undergoes his training analysis not
merely to acquire technical competence in the use of the

method, but in order to increase his maturity as a human being. It is accepted that before one can have the right or the capacity to seek to help one's fellows to maturity, one must have attained a reasonable degree of maturity oneself. Evidently then the practice of psychoanalysis for psychotherapeutic purposes rests on the acceptance of maturity of personality as a value. One *ought* to desire to be a mature person, and one *ought* to take whatever steps lie in one's power to become a mature person. Why? The question is not answered for the analyst by saying that it is necessary if he is to help his patients to become mature persons, for why should the patient oblige the analyst by himself desiring to become mature? Why does he not banish his neurotic illness by repressing or defying his guilty feelings and becoming openly aggressive, delinquent or criminal instead of being ill? *In order that psychotherapy may be carried on at all, both the therapist and the patient must in the long run accept maturity of personality as a value that carries obligation with it.* The patient who has no sense of values and no principles, if he starts analysis at all, is quite likely to call a halt as soon as he feels somewhat better, refuse to look beyond the relief of symptoms and discomforts, and may be to depart without paying the analyst's fees. He will feel little more than resentment at having had to bother with the business at all, has no sense of responsibility to the analyst (who has to live by his work like other people), and may disappear as many people do when they move house and leave their tradesmen's bills unpaid. Clearly for the serious pursuit of psychotherapy, values are important on both sides. The fact that the above situation is only a rare occasional occurrence and it is general for analyst and patient to part on terms of mutual respect and regard shows that values are in fact accepted.

There are many people who would never resort to psychotherapy, because they feel no sort of responsibility for solving their problems by undergoing any change in themselves. There is a marked tendency nowadays to substitute the term 'mental health' for 'maturity of personality'. This is certainly due to

164

the desire to find a more 'scientific' and morally neutral term in our scientific age. But the implication of 'value' is not really avoided, for why should anyone trouble about becoming mentally healthy if he can get along to his own satisfaction by riding roughshod over other people instead, as Hitler and his Nazis and all political and financial thugs do?

The bulk of the present chapter originally formed the substance of a University lecture on *Mental Health and Values*[1] which was itself a sign of the times. The lecture came at the end of a short series devoted primarily to the scientific approach to human personality. Professor Arnold Toynbee, in his 1953 Gifford Lectures, referred to the fact that in the seventeenth century European man had turned away from religion to science. I quote from the report in *The Scotsman*:

'Today the time has come for us to follow this seventeenth-century example of jumping clear in our turn from the mathematical-physical standpoint that has armed mankind with deadly weapons without having redeemed it from Original Sin. We need once again to make a new start— and this time by returning to the spiritual outlook that was abandoned in the seventeenth century. But in doing this we must take care not to repeat our seventeenth-century ancestors' mistake. They threw away religion itself in their anxiety to get rid of the evils of religious strife and warfare. In now seeking to retrieve the religion they discarded, we do not have to throw away the technological and scientific achievements of the last quarter of a millenium. We merely need to realize that technology is not either a cure for sin or a key to the mystery of the universe (*The Scotsman*, Nov. 1953).

For our present purpose I shall discard specifically theological terms since we are concerned to understand human nature and experience on the psychological level. Therefore instead of 'original sin' (a controversial term anyway) I shall substitute 'personality disorder' or 'mental ill health', which may manifest itself in anti-social behaviour as an alternative

[1] At University College, Hull, Dec. 1953.

to neurotic illness. I shall also discard for the moment the term 'religion' as distinct from 'science' and use the more general term 'spiritual outlook' as distinct from 'scientific outlook'. This serves to remind us that religion and science are not separate, opposed and self-contained entities existing *per se* but distinct, though correlated, attitudes and activities of men. Values are primarily matters of spiritual or personal perception unless we are thinking of purely utilitarian values. Values as such are not scientific concerns except as facts of human experience open to psychological investigation, for science makes an impersonal non-valuing approach to all phenomena. I would say then that it is profoundly true that the time has come for us to transcend without discarding the purely technological, mechanistic, scientific approach to man. The double approach is needed today. Four centuries of the gospel of science find us in an even worse plight than the seventeenth century, in a world racked by hatred after the two worst wars of all time, and labouring under the shadow of a third possible war on an atomic scale. It is clear that science has done no more than give us tools. We still have to settle the question 'In the service of what values shall we use them?' We can only settle that by returning once more to the spiritual approach to man, though retaining possession of the achievements of technology and science at the same time. We may not now be unscientific, but neither may we be nothing but scientific.

Once more, for our present purposes, I want to substitute for the term 'spiritual approach' the more manageable term 'personal approach', since this brings out clearly just where the mechanistic scientific point of view falls short of being adequate. Our problems today are not on the level of technical competence but on the level of personality and personal relationships. Now, pure science ties us down to a mechanistic approach to human personality, and the plain fact is that we just cannot deal satisfactorily on that level with all that is involved in the 'person' and 'personal relationships'. *Persons act from motives, not from mechanistic causes, and motives and values are bound up together. Science has nothing to do with value per se.*

Science has no values except its own narrowly scientific ones, which I would not dignify by the name of 'truth' but would call simply 'accuracy', since so much of the full range of truth lies outside the field of interest of pure science.

There is not really any cause for dispute in all this, provided the scientist is humble and does not set up to be an arbiter of what lies beyond his own legitimate field of interest. If, however, he is arrogant and claims that only the pure scientific approach to reality matters and everything else is vague and useless speculation, then he must be sharply challenged. The importance of this is evident when we reflect that some will say that our present troubles are due to the fact that science has not yet been fully applied to human nature and we want more science, not a different approach. But what is meant by applying science to human nature? That depends on whether you hold a narrower or broader view of science. A case in point is that of Dr. H. J. Eysenck who, in his Pelican book on *The Uses and Abuses of Psychology*, takes the narrow view and makes a somewhat hostile attack on psychotherapy. Much of what he says about the need for scientific testing and validation of psychotherapeutic results merits careful attention. The psychotherapeutic process is a proper object of scientific study. However, Eysenck shows little realistic grasp of what psychotherapy is all about, and little appreciation of the fact that it is the personal, motivated lives of human beings that we are dealing with when we try to promote mental health. *The Times Literary Supplement* reviewer of his book took him to task for this as follows:

'His account of abnormal psychology is so wide of the mark as to be seriously misleading to the lay reader, and infuriating to the specialist in psychological medicine. . . . (The book is) marred by a strident insistence on the author's scientific purity altogether out of keeping with the traditional spirit of scientific humility.'

The reviewer ends by quoting a character of George Orwell who goes to sleep murmuring 'Sanity is not statistical.'

Eysenck is an example of what happens when the limitations of science are forgotten. He makes it clear that he is really concerned to discredit psychotherapy in favour of what he calls scientific therapy, which turns out to be quite mechanistic in orientation. He regards what he calls '*habits* of emotional maladjustment' as the 'nucleus of a neurosis', and mechanistic 'habit-breaking' devices as the really scientific method of dealing with it. He concedes to psychotherapy a minor rôle, and writes: 'The most useful part for psychotherapy to play may not be as a *substitute* for these more fundamental methods but rather as an *adjunct*. Some of the writers who have used habit-breaking methods of the type described here have added a statement to the effect that in their view psycho-therapy should accompany the treatment.' But since Eysenck regards psychotherapy as quite unscientific he cannot really allow it any validity from his point of view. He does not seem to recognize that his own comment on this quite gives the show away. He says about this adjunctive use of psycho-therapy: 'There are stresses and strains arising in the breaking of any firmly anchored habit which may require the help of an outsider, as they would otherwise be beyond the patient's ability to bear without impairing his nervous stability' (op. cit. pp. 219–20). Exactly. These scientific habit-breaking devices merely remove symptoms, and when that is done the patient's personal problems, anxiety, conflict, stress and strain as an individual person, promptly emerge as we saw in Chapter II, and, even on Eysenck's own admission, we have to fall back on psychotherapy at this point.

So far as Eysenck is concerned, he appears to have quite given up any real attempt to understand human beings in their dynamic emotional development as individual persons. He writes:

'Many of the greatest psychologists are, if anything, below average in this quality of "insight" into human motives and purposes.... The expectation frequently voiced, namely that psychologists should have learned a lot about "human nature" ... is quite unjustified. The psychologist knows no more about "human nature" than the next man, and if he is wise he will not let his claims outrun his discretion. If the psychologist as a scientist is not trying to understand other people, then what precisely is he trying to do? He is trying to explain their conduct in terms of a system of general scientific laws' (op. cit. pp. 224–5).

That is commendably clear. Eysenck distinguishes between 'understanding' and 'explaining' and says that psychotherapy and psychoanalysis are only concerned to understand, but science is concerned to explain. However, this scientific explanation is, on his own admission, entirely valueless to help us to understand better what human beings are about, and when scientific habit-breaking has been accomplished, we must after all fall back on, psychotherapy to deal with the disturbing personal problems that then emerge. Personally, I would rank the understanding of human beings in their personal life as on a far higher level of importance and usefulness than Dr. Eysenck's somewhat sterile scientific explaining. He presents us with the dilemma of accepting his narrow view of science and admitting that 'understanding human nature' is entirely outside its purview, or else broadening our conception of science. Psychoanalysts will not, I think, be very perturbed at his view that psychoanalysis is not scientific because it only aims at understanding. Must we accept Eysenck's narrow view of science as fundamentally mechanistic in its approach and not personal? If so, the individual person and living personal relationships are outside the scope of scientific study. It must be stressed that 'personality', which Dr. Eysenck specializes in studying scientifically, is an abstraction, and is not at all the same thing as a living, functioning, motivated person who needs to be understood and cannot be accounted for solely by 'general scientific laws'. Rather than accept the rigidly mechanistic view of science, it is better to recognize that science must be understood in a narrower and also in a broader way. The narrow view is appropriate to mathematics, physics, chemistry, etc. The broader view is needed if we are to speak of sociological sciences. When science comes to study 'the person', altogether subtler concepts are needed such as make it possible to concede scientific status to psychoanalysis. As Professor Macmurray maintains, philosophy has not yet worked out the concepts by means of which science can deal with the personal life (*Interpreting the Universe*, p. 122). Psychotherapy is a field in which scientific investigation and testing, and the personal therapeutic approach must learn to work together with mutual respect, and not with the one-sidedness and antagonism that Eysenck manifests.

Instead of treating patients as persons whose troubles and conflicts lie in the region of motives and purposes, he treats them as bundles of habits which must be corrected by scientific devices based on what he calls a new psychology of learning. These methods of scientific therapy, however, turn out not to be so new after all. They boil down to three: the reconditioning of conditioned reflexes, habit substitution, and suggestion. For the first he cites an electrical device for waking up the nocturnal enuretic when he wants to pass water, for the second the substitution of chewing gum for cigarettes, and for the third, post-hypnotic suggestion and curing children of nail-biting by playing gramophone records giving appropriate suggestions while they sleep. *Why* the patient passes water in his sleep, or smokes compulsively, or bites his nails does not apparently matter. So long as you scientifically put a stop to these tension-relieving symptomatic activities, the nature of the tensions seems to be irrelevant. That might perhaps be relegated to psychotherapy as an adjunct to these 'more fundamental methods'.

This really would be comic if it were not tragic. It is a mere 'symptom-therapy', a collection of natty little tricks to cure nasty little tics. In addition the patient may be put through a series of objective tests to establish that he scores, say, 75 per cent constitutional neuroticism, and we can do very little about it.

Dr. Eysenck has depersonalized the human person and excluded motives. The need to love and be loved, the fact of love embittered to a choking, stifling hate by frustration of all really human needs, hopes and goals, these are facts that are far more important and momentous than the annoying symptomatic habits that Eysenck's therapy cures. If science 'explaining conduct in terms of a system of general scientific laws' cannot deal with this urgent personal life of man, then, though we need not discard science within its own legitimate field, we must transcend its mechanistic point of view. This is what we are doing when we talk about mental health and values.

Eysenck regards psychoanalysis as unscientific,

'because all reactions whatever can be explained . . . even if none can be predicted. However, it is not *ex post facto* explanation which constitutes science, but prediction which can be verified . . . Concepts like reaction-formation are essentially *ad hoc* hypotheses which inevitably explain the individual case because they have been put forward to explain it, but which do not fit into any systematic framework . . . if we make up an *ad hoc* hypothesis for every new case—which essentially is the method of psychoanalysis—then we shall never go beyond the present position where we can explain everything and predict nothing' (1953, p. 235).

This is an interesting passage. What he is complaining of is that psychoanalytic psychotherapy deals with the patient as an individual, i.e. a person. Mechanistic science of Eysenck's type cannot deal with the individual person except by depersonalizing him and 'fitting him into a systematic framework'. He wants to treat individual persons as members of a class, and as mechanisms whose action can be predicted. He says that psychoanalytic concepts do not 'help us in deciding between a number of possible alternatives' (1953, p. 235) as to the future action of the individual. It seems that Eysenck believes that such predictive decision is possible, but in 'human action' it is the individual person who decided what he will do, and no science will ever be able to predict beforehand how he will decide. Prediction, except in rough and ready ways based on broad understanding, is the one thing that is *not* possible in dealing with individual persons. Either the 'individual person' will remain forever outside science in Eysenck's narrow view of science, or else his view of science must be broadened to take in the study of individual personality. Professor Arnold Toynbee, as we saw, in his recent Gifford Lecture stated it as his view that, whereas in the seventeenth-century Europe abandoned religion and turned to science, it is now time that we rose above the mathematical, physical and technological point of view, and without abandoning science recovered the religious approach to man, not necessarily in the seventeenth-century sense. I agree that *mechanistic* science cannot deal with human persons as such.

Eysenck defines psychotherapy as 'a systematic . . . exploration of a neurotic patient's mental processes by verbal means' (op. cit., p. 195), i.e. as an investigatory process. A pure scientist would naturally look at it that way. That is a definition, not of psychotherapy, but of psychoanalysis as a research method. No one is ever cured by an investigation. In personal problems people are only cured by a therapeutic personal relationship. We might compare a psychoneurosis to a vitamin-deficiency disease which is cured by supplying the missing vitamins. Good personal relationships are the life-giving vitamins of personal development. The bad results of their lack cannot be cured merely by an investigation of those results but only by supplying what is missing. I would say that psychotherapy of the psychoanalytic type is giving the patient an opportunity (which he may use, misuse, or refuse to use) to work over with another person all his difficulties in personal relationships so that he may have a chance of solving them in an atmosphere of patient understanding, and so grow more mature. In the process he becomes conscious, sometimes spontaneously, at others with the analyst's help, of aims and attitudes he did not know he had, and of what sets them up and keeps them going. So he gains a chance to relinquish them in the more realistic situation of the analytical relationship. The patient is inwardly bound to that side of his parents on which personal relationships broke down, so that he is a person who is cut off and isolated by starved needs, hates and fears. His early life has left him with little or nothing in himself to build on. Psychotherapy is his struggle to break through these inhibiting barriers and get in touch with the therapist as one person to another, in a realistic appropriate way, so as to become more capable of relationship in his real outer life.

It is as well to remind ourselves again that science and scientific methods are neutral from the point of view of values, and may be used for good and also for bad purposes. The techniques for habit-breaking and re-conditioning that Dr. Eysenck relies on in preference to human understanding and the personal approach, may also put power into the hands of political dictators who want to re-condition human beings in the light of their particular system of values. Robert Waelder in *Psychoanalysis and Culture*, remarks that 'the methods of totalitarians operate as a scientific break-up of human nature', which should give us pause and bring us back from science to values. What science can do is to tell us how to do something from a technical point of view. Whether we want to do it, and still more whether we ought to want to do it is another matter. I will go so far as to say that a person who has no proper values or whose values are destructive is not a mentally healthy person.

To begin with, we have already remarked that *mental health is itself a value*. We do not, for example, regard a thoroughly aggressive person as mentally healthy. We have come to regard him, as a result of psychoanalytical investigations which even Dr. Eysenck quotes (op. cit., p. 272), as an example of the authoritarian and basically sado-masochistic personality. Suppose we say to him: 'You are not a mentally healthy person. We will give you psychotherapy, or else we will scientifically break up these unhealthy habits and recondition you.' He will reply, no doubt in choice language of his own, 'No, you won't. You can keep your mental health. I'd rather go on exploiting people for my own ends.' Because of that, very aggressive people are a poor prospect for psychotherapy because they do not want it, and do not submit to it, in fact they hardly ever seek it. *Only those who regard mental health as a value seek it*, for mental health can only be understood at the level of the personal life and personal relationships, where disturbed reactions are not just bad habits to be mechanistically explained and corrected, but have complex personal significances, and embody aims and purposes which imply false and unhealthy values.

Mental health from the human point of view can only be defined in terms of values. We believe that a mature person who can be patient under opposition, firm against attack, but magnanimous to opponents, affectionate and loyal in personal relationships, and free from morbid fears and guilts, is mentally healthier than a hate-ridden, revengeful, neurotically aggressive sadist, or a compliant, timid, pleasing, but secretly self-pitying and resentful person who exploits illness to control other people. In other words, our very criteria for distinguishing mature from neurotic are 'value-judgments' implying that some types and characteristics of persons are good and others are bad.

Psychotherapy leans heavily on values even though it does not make a moralistic approach to a patient. A cynical, disillusioned person who has no faith in anything, and whose universal scepticism leaves him with nothing positive to live for, is not only in a very unhealthy state of mind, but he is also a poor therapeutic prospect. A person has little chance of solving personal problems with psychotherapeutic or any other help unless he has incentives strong enough to make him feel it is worth while to go through the mental pains involved in growing personality changes. The people who offer the best prospects for psychotherapy are those who, in spite of their conflicts, anxieties and symptoms, retain a conviction that it really does matter that we should be more and not less mature, that maturity of character is intrinsically valuable and ought to be striven for.

It is true that most patients begin psychotherapy with only utilitarian aims in mind. They want to get rid of distressing symptoms, or seek rehabilitation as wage-earners. That will only suffice to carry a patient part of the way in psychoanalytic psychotherapy, for sooner or later he must come up against the fundamental problem that the real issue at stake is what kind of a person he is. In my experience a patient must believe in higher values than these utilitarian ones before he feels it to be worthwhile to stick at the process of radical personality change, and the overcoming of hate in favour of love within himself.

I would like now to pave the way for raising the question of the definition of values, that is from the point of view of mental health, not of philosophical enquiry. I think we may do this by asking what difference psychoanalysis has made to our approach to values.

The older pre-psychoanalytical position was the orthodox religious and moral traditional position. The human being was an eternal soul and as such was free and self-determining. He could choose between good and evil, and the values he was required to choose were absolute, intrinsic, and eternal like himself. Discipline and training were necessary to ensure that the child should choose the right values, and he was punished by parents, and later by society, if he did not respond.

An opposite position as a reaction grew up under the influence of the social sciences. The sociological, anthropological and cultural view revived the teaching of the ancient Greek Sophists, that of the relativity of all values. It was said that what we mean by the right values was merely the values that obtained in our own cultural and social group. What was regarded as valuable in one culture might well be considered worthless in another. Values are historically and locally determined and there are no absolute values. You can, therefore, act on your own private notions of value if you can get enough people to agree with you (as the Nazis and Fascists did), or alternately if you are prepared to pay the price of social disapproval. There is no real question of right or wrong involved, for these terms cease to have much meaning. There is much that is true and more that is only plausible in this point of view. I am sure the critical and comparative studies of the specific institutional values of different cultures by cultural anthropologists has been itself valuable. It is an antidote to stuffiness, parochialism, and obscurantism.

It must, however, be noted that the theory of the relativity of specific values does not destroy the concept of value *per se*. Values are clearly an indispensable part of human living, for however much their detailed definition may change from one group to another, all human groups find it necessary to regard some qualities of character, some actions, some objects, as worth more than others. Human beings are incapable of conducting their lives except on the assumption that value is a real thing. We have to discover how to distinguish between the 'essence' and the 'accidental cultural forms' of values.

This is no new problem. Professor Toynbee raised the same problem with regard to religion in the Gifford Lectures already quoted. Again quoting the press report in *The Scotsman*, Professor Toynbee said that:

'The heritage of each of the higher religions was a combination of two elements. Each contains essential counsels and truths valid at all times and places, and also non-essential accessories, accidentally acquired in the course of the religion's transit through time and space. These accidental accretions were the price that the eternal and universal essence of a higher religion had to pay for communicating itself to the members of a particular human society at a particular stage in that society's history. . . . The task of disengaging the essence of a religion from its accidents was therefore one that needed to be carried out again and again . . . though this task was as hazardous as it was indispensable' (*The Scotsman*, Nov. 14, 1953).

The same must be said about the problem of values in general. We would expect that in different circumstances values will take on different local complexions. That does not really lead to the doctrine of the essential relativity of all value, which actually undermines the concept of value altogether and reduces it to mere personal taste and preference.

This so-called scientific view that values are merely matters of individual private opinion has received a rude jolt of recent years, as is illustrated by the psychoanalyst, R. Money-Kyrle. In *Psychoanalysis and Politics* he writes:

'Moral statements, so it was argued, were either concealed definitions or expressions of preference, and in neither case susceptible of proof. Therefore the judgment of each individual's conscience . . . could be dismissed as the accidental products of the cultural environment in which he happened to be reared. And social anthropology, by pointing to a great variety of codes to be found in different cultures, seemed to support this view. The Ethical Relativist who holds it renounces all claims to judge other people's moral standards and is rather apologetic about his own which he regards as an acquired if ineradicable prejudice. This is a congenial doctrine to a disillusioned generation. . . . The swing from Ethical Absolutism to Ethical Relativism was completed by about 1925. . . . But it was soon most rudely challenged by the rise of a new, or the revival of an archaic, code in Italy and Germany, which demanded a fanatical obedience to a leader and an unbounded ruthlessness towards whatever he regarded as an enemy. As the Ethical Relativist read of the brutal and progressive extirpation of all freedom in fascist countries, he became aware of an increasing moral indignation rise within himself. Yet his theory told him that Mussolini's or Hitler's morals were, from their point of view, as valid as his own from his. In common with my generation I had been influenced by these successive attitudes to morals which followed and contradicted each other in so short a space of time. The last —that of Ethical Relativism—had become emotionally untenable. (pp. 8–9).

I find it hard to understand why a psychoanalyst should have had to wait for the rise of totalitarian tyranny and brutality before seeing that Ethical Relativism, in any sense that undermined the reality of moral values, was untenable.

There were enough evils lying at our very doors in society and visible to the analyst in the unconscious, to teach that any day. However, we might now say that the *Modern Position* is more one of consciousness of a need for clear and definite values, than of confidence in the possession of them. But I believe there is much to be said for Money-Kyrle's contention that a rigorous psychoanalytical investigation of the difference between mature and immature types of personality and character can provide us with an objective means of establishing at any rate some basic moral values. What has been the impact of psychoanalysis hitherto on this question? So far it has not been of much help. It has done much to debunk inadequate conceptions of value but not much to establish new ones, as Erich Fromm maintained. He writes:

'In order to know what is good or bad for man one has to know the nature of man. They are, therefore, also fundamentally psychological enquiries. . . . Psychoanalysis should have been one of the most potent stimuli for the development of humanistic ethics. But while psychoanalysis has tremendously increased our knowledge of man, it has not increased our knowledge of how man ought to live and what he ought to do. Its main function has been one of "debunking", of demonstrating that value judgments and ethical norms are the rationalized expressions of irrational —and often unconscious desires and fears and that they therefore have no claim to objective validity. While this debunking was exceedingly valuable in itself, it became increasingly sterile when it failed to go beyond mere criticism. Psychoanalysis, in an attempt to establish psychology as a natural science, made the mistake of divorcing psychology from problems of philosophy and ethics. It ignored the fact that human personality can not be understood unless we look at man in his totality, which included his need to find an answer to the question of the meaning of his existence and to discover norms according to which he ought to live. . . . The character structure of the mature and integrated personality, the productive character, constitutes the source and the basis of "virtue" ' (*Man for Himself*, pp. 6–7).

I cannot regard it as adequate when Fromm says that 'neurosis itself is, in the last analysis, a symptom of moral failure', but I can agree that 'the success of the therapeutic effort depends on the understanding and solution of the person's moral problem' (op. cit., p. viii). 'The understanding of man's nature and the understanding of values and norms for his life are interdependent' (idem). What Fromm says of earlier psychoanalysis applies with even greater force to the pure psychology of Eysenck which tries to explain man solely from the mechanistic point of view and leaves out his personal life. Money-Kyrle set himself to remedy the earlier failure of psychoanalysis to develop the concept of 'maturity' with sufficient clarity to give help in redefining or confirming the basic human values. Values cannot be dismissed as mere defences against, and compensations for, anti-social un-conscious, infantile trends. Such defences are vitally necessary if we are not to relapse into barbarism. If a man has sadistic murderous impulses it is as well that he should feel enough guilt to make him repress them, and stop him from murdering people. These defences spring from our perception of the need to grow up to the kind of maturity that makes good human relationships possible, and if you break down all defences there is nothing left but emotional and moral chaos. *Moral values are our perception of, and our loyalty to, those qualities of mature personality that are necessary if we are to sustain constructive and not destructive human relationships.* Psychotherapy aims at bringing the individual to that maturity, so that values do not need to be forcibly imposed on him by society or a strict super-ego, but express his own genuine feelings and desires, and freely developed capacity to love.

The question of whether psychoanalysis has a destructive effect on moral values is often raised by patients in the earlier stages of treatment when they are encountering their initial difficulties about it, and resistances to accepting it. A patient may confess, with marked feelings of guilt, to being unjustifiably bad tempered, or to feeling jealous and envious towards other people. He will say: 'This is shocking. I feel very ashamed of it. I ought to crush down such feelings and I try my best to do so. I feel I'm a horrible person.' Gradually he becomes aware that the analyst does not share his punitive and harshly repressive attitude towards himself and does not think badly of him for having to struggle with such problems in himself. For a long time he cannot accept the analyst's point of view. He will probably say: 'You don't blame me openly because its your business to try to help me, but you must really think badly of me in your mind and you're too polite to say so.'

The analyst, however, patiently refuses to blame and goes on trying to understand. In proportion as the patient has relied on the moral defence to control what he could not alter in himself, he may grow anxious if he cannot rope the analyst in to aid his defences by inveigling him into judgment and moral disapproval. Still the analyst takes the line not of condemning, but of trying to help the patient to discover why he gets so angry or jealous. Where do these offending impulses come from? What first set up these tendencies? When have you felt like this before? What keeps it all going now? Then the patient may say: 'But you excuse everything, you explain everything away, you make it seem as if there's no difference between right and wrong, you seem to destroy all moral values.'

The answer to these doubts and fears is quite definite. The patient's sense of moral values must not be weakened or undermined. The fact that he feels guilty about his anti-social trends is part of his motivation for wanting to change them. If he could not feel guilty, psychotherapy would become virtually impossible. The capacity for feeling guilty about hurting other people is part of a socialized personality and in itself a mature thing. Nevertheless, guilt is dangerous because it can spring from a morbid inability to be angry with other people at all, even when anger is justified. It is so often a highly destructive in-turning of all anger which sets up depressed states of mind and undermines the personality. Guilty feeling is often the sign that moral values are being used, not as standards for guidance and ideals for inspiration, to make clear the goal at which we all seek to arrive but as a stick to beat oneself with. Moral condemnation, as distinct from the affirmation of moral values, is very usually a disguised way of venting aggression both against other people and oneself. This is clear when it rises to the pitch of moral indignation, which, whether it be expressed against others or oneself, is an exceedingly suspect reaction as to its real motives.

I usually explain to the patient three things:

(a) That his guilt is a good thing in so far as it is a sensitiveness to other people's hurts and a desire to change; but a dangerous thing in so far as it is a persisting, wearing, nagging, destructive attack on himself.

(b) That to seek to explain and understand is not the same thing as excusing, and the ignoring of moral values. It rather presupposes moral values and a desire to change. An anti-social action is still anti-social, but when we understand how and why a person feels the impulse to it, it becomes possible to grow out of it.

(c) That to condemn a feeling does nothing to help cure or change it. At best it only represses it, and thereby preserves it. When people cannot alter or control anti-social impulses to kill, steal, exploit, etc. then the law, basing its action on the moral standards of the community, must step in and enforce control. But that is a punitive and preventive measure which suppresses without changing the criminal in all of us. Every modern prison administration seeks to do more than that. Psychoanalysis seeks to draw into consciousness the whole underlying and sustaining motivational structure of the bad impulse, to help the patient to grow out of the inner tie to past bad situations that first created it: but moral values abide.

We may now say a few words about values of three kinds: aesthetic, moral and spiritual.

Aesthetic Values. I shall here merely summarize a view set forth by W. R. D. Fairbairn of Edinburgh. Art, like dreams, deals in symbolism, and symbolism expresses the dynamic emotional and impulsive life of the unconscious in ways that are acceptable to, and promote the health of, the waking conscious self. It deals, therefore, with the fundamental emotional problems of the personal life—love and hate, fear and anger, destructiveness and reparative constructiveness, anxiety and guilt. It allows our deep unconscious reactions to life to find an expression in consciousness and so counteracts blind repression. At the same time it gives them expression in such a way as to enable us to feel that blind, destructive urges can be controlled and offset by re-creative urges which cancel out the destruction; thus it allays guilt. Art relieves repression, allays guilt and gives vigorous outlet to dynamic forces in man, for things may be done in art that may not be done in social action. It thus promotes mental health in so far as it has true aesthetic value. To put that the other way round, it has true aesthetic value in so far as it promotes mental health. It only does this under the condition that the artistic product is neither oversymbolized nor undersymbolized. If the art is oversymbolized, it becomes conventional, tame, uninspiring, unmoving, because not enough dynamic unconscious material breaks through to give it force. It does nothing then to release the unconscious, but becomes a party as it were to repression. On the other hand, if the art is undersymbolized it becomes too disturbing. Unconscious material breaks through with all too little disguise, and may at best seem crude and at worst horrifying and frankly psychotic, as with some of the surrealists and more bizarre moderns. Obviously the optimum balance between over- and under-symbolization, that is between repression and release of the unconscious, differs for different persons, for the same person at different times, and certainly for different periods of history and culture. There are times when we get too tame and conventional, and need to be disturbed by less disguised expressions of the primitive life-forces in us. There are other times when individuals and also cultures are already too disturbed and need help in stabilizing their emotional forces. Art does not necessarily always have the same job to do in aiding mental health. That is why aesthetic values are so relative and subjective. What has artistic value for one person, has little for another. We cannot, therefore, define aesthetic values in a specific way but they contribute greatly to mental health. You might call this the utilitarian aspect of aesthetic values. They must have in addition spiritual aspects which are inherent in imaginative creativeness, and serve to heighten the sense of the meaningfulness of human living: for the artist himself his work has significance as a creative expression of his personality.

Moral Values. These are pre-eminently an expression of aspects of good human relationship. Moral values may be defined as emerging in the attitudes and behaviour of a mature person to other persons in all the many and varied relationships of life. These range from casual contacts in which at least courtesy is required, through all kinds of co-operative activities which call for mutual understanding, consideration, and loyalty, up to, finally, the most intimate relationships of life-long love and partnership. Moral values appear in recreational, social, economic and political activity; the extent to which they are embodied in behaviour as a natural self-expression rather than as an enforced code of rules is an indication of the maturity of the person. Properly speaking, moral values express the intrinsic good qualities of human living in personal relationships. Like aesthetic values, however, they also have a utilitarian aspect. Fairbairn speaks of 'the moral defence' against repressed unconscious anti-social drives, and the defensive aspect of moral values, in which the claim we recognize they have on us strengthens our inner resistance to dangerous immature trends, is of supreme importance to society. The loss of this 'super-ego' controlling function of moral values would lay us open to barbarism and undermine all that we mean by a civilized way of living. But it is a moral value that we should not use our moral values as a means of angry attack on others or as a means of enforcing an intimidating discipline on children.

One of the points at which our traditional moral values need to be corrected is the one-sidedness of self-denying and self-abnegating ideals. A well-known Christian hymn ends the first verse with the words 'All of self and none of Thee', and closes the last verse with the exact reversal of that position, in the words 'None of self and all of Thee'. Psychoanalysis has enabled us to see the extreme danger of this denial of all rights to self. It cripples the full creative spontaneity and expression of the individual self, and leads to non-fulfilment and loss of creative gifts by inhibition. Psychoanalysis has thus brought us back to the New Testament dictum, 'Thou shalt love the Lord thy God . . . and thy neighbour as thyself' (Mt. xix, 19, Mk. xii, 31, Lk. x, 27, Rom. xiii, 9, Jas. ii, 8). We must regard it as immoral to deny to ourselves those rights that are important for the proper development and expression of our own full nature. These rights must of course be balanced by the consideration of the rights of other people to similar treatment, but 'rights' do not constitute a oneway traffic. Particularly when children are brought up to feel that they have no rights over against the grown-ups, and are only there to fit in and not be a nuisance, a severe crippling of personality can result. It is important to see that people who cannot value and love their own self in a constructive way are not able to love other people.

Spiritual Values. I shall not say much about these at this point because the subject belongs to the next chapter. Nevertheless, there are values that are of supreme importance to healthy living, to full self-realization, and to a constructive contribution to our human environment, that can only be called 'spiritual'. They transcend both aesthetic and moral values. They arise out of whatever answer we give to such questions as 'What is the ultimate meaning and purpose of our existence?' 'What do we really live for in the end?' They emerge in the statement of those intrinsic elements of quality in human personality and personal relationship which make these things 'ends in themselves'. This opens up the whole question of religious faith which we shall consider in Chapter XII. I will content myself here with quoting a few lines from Professor John Macmurray's *Reason and Emotion*.

'The personal life demands a relationship in which we can be our whole selves and have complete freedom to express everything that makes us what we are. It demands a relationship with one another in which suppression and inhibition are unnecessary. Friendship, fellowship, communion, love ... are ... the idea of a relationship between us which has no purpose beyond itself; in which we associate because it is natural for human beings to share their experience, to understand one another, and to find joy and satisfaction in living together; in expressing and revealing themselves to one another. If one asks why people form friendships and love one another the question is simply unanswerable. We can only say, because it is the nature of persons to do so. They can only be themselves that way.... This is the characteristic of personal relationships. They have no ulterior motive.... Their value lies entirely in themselves, and for the same reason transcends all other values' (pp. 98, 99, 101).

According to Macmurray:

'Religion ... is the force which creates friendship, society, community, co-operation in living.... The promise of the full maturity of religion in human life is put perfectly in St. Paul's words: "Then shall I know even as also I am known"' (op. cit. pp. 62–3).

Religion has always insisted that all this is consummated and perfected in one supreme relationship which links man as a person with the ultimate reality conceived as personal and experienced as God. As St. Augustine put it: 'Thou hast made us for Thyself and our hearts are restless until they find rest in Thee' (*Confessions*). Spiritual values appear to define the intrinsic worth of good personal relationship and are reached out towards in Plato's 'Idea of the Good', in the philosopher's 'summum bonum', in St. Paul's 'the greatest of these is love', and in the New Testment basis of personal religion, 'God is love'.

CHAPTER XII

Psychotherapy and Religion

In the last chapter we saw reason to affirm that psychotherapy rests on values, and that it does not weaken and undermine but rather preserves and confirms values. When successful in leading to a true maturity of the person it enables him to live out his values in a relatively natural and effortless way, so that he is released from the harsh and anxious tyranny of a compulsive morality. In psychotherapeutic practice this would be described as the transformation of an obsessional or a depressed person into a mature and truly loving personality. We saw that psychotherapy, being a dynamic personal relationship and a process of personality development, is not itself a scientific activity. It can and should be scientifically studied, and the knowledge gained used to help the process. Psychotherapy itself, however, while it uses a scientific technique for discovering problems, is an exercise of a personal healing influence by one human being on another, making possible the growth of confidence, faith and hope, and cancelling out past destructive influences. It is an arena in which scientific observations can be made. The analyst is therapist and scientist at the same time but the rôles are not confused.

Thus Fairbairn has stated uncompromisingly that what the patient needs is 'salvation' (*Brit. J. Med. Psych.*, Vol. xxviii 1955, p. 156), the saving of his crushed and devitalized ego from the destructive power of undermining past experiences perpetuated in his mental make-up in the form of internalized bad objects and the destructive emotions and impulses they arouse in him, and the often equally self-destructive defences he is obliged to build up within himself. This brings us face to face with the religious problem and the question of the wide range of psychotherapeutic agencies in everyday life itself.

Psychology as a science is not concerned with the ultimate truth of religion. Psychology likewise cannot pronounce on the nature and real objective existence of the material objects of sense-perception, for even as a science its business is not the investigation of the objects but of the mental experience of perceiving. The scientific investigation of material objects is the business of physics, chemistry and other such sciences, while the question of their existence apart from the perceiving mind is ultimately a question for philosophy. So also neither can psychology pronounce on the nature and real objective existence of the object or objects of the religious consciousness. In this case there can be no science concerned with their direct investigation and the question of their nature and real existence is again a question for philosophy. Psychology can only deal with the nature of religious experience. Here we are particularly concerned with the problem of the psychotherapeutic possibilities of religious experience.

Whatever metaphysical battles are waged over the question of the objective reality or meaning of God and 'the supernatural', religious experience is one of the great outstanding facts of human history right back into prehistoric ages. Further, the reality and power of the psychotherapeutic effect of religious experience under certain conditions is a fact. These facts call to be studied from the scientific, psychological point of view. But other aspects of human experience also prove, in practice, to have psychotherapeutic power and religion does not stand alone in this respect. It may, however, well be true that it is a broadly religious aspect of such experiences as friendship, marriage, devotion to a great and worthy cause, creative work, etc., that endows them with psychotherapeutic power and value. This is what we have to look into, and we shall naturally not be concerned with propaganda in favour of particular forms of religious 'church' or 'faith' but with the essence of religion as such.

Since psychotherapy is not a purely impersonal, scientific,

technical activity but a matter of the healing power of good human relationship, it must have wide ramifications. It cannot be confined to a professional, specialized form of treatment even though the development of a specialized psychotherapy based on knowledge scientifically discovered is essential. Such professional psychotherapy, so far as the essential therapeutic factor is concerned, has an unbroken continuity with all the healing agencies of life in general and should never be allowed to become divorced from life in general, for it has much both to give to, and to receive from, the general experience of mankind of the power of good personal relationships both to allay anxiety and to promote growth towards maturity. Unless ordinary human relationships in general had an all-important psychotherapeutic power, anxiety would have destroyed the human race long ago. This fact of the psychotherapeutic power of good personal relationships operates over the widest possible range of human experience and is in fact co-extensive with life itself.

Since in the beginning the healthy and harmonious development of the infant as a person depends on his being provided with a mentally healthy and loving human environment, such an environment must promote mental health at every stage of human life. Karen Horney writes:

'Life itself is the most effective help for our development. The hardships that life forces upon us—a necessity to leave one's country, organic illness, periods of solitude and also its gifts—a good friendship, even a mere contact with a truly good and valuable human being, co-operative work in groups—all such factors can help us to reach our full potential. Unfortunately, the assistance thus offered has certain disadvantages: the beneficent factors do not always come at the time we need them; the hardships may not only be a challenge to our activity and courage but surpass our available strength and merely crush us; finally, we may be too entangled in psychic difficulties to be able to utilize the help offered by life. Since psychoanalysis has not these disadvantages—though it has others—it can legitimately take its place as one specific means in the service of personal development' (*Self Analysis*, 1942, pp. 8–9).

The important point is here clearly put that psychoanalysis takes its place as a special part of the general developing and healing function of the whole of our life in relationship with one another. There can be no doubt that many people are saved from a nervous breakdown which otherwise would have come to them by the fact that they were fortunate in their choice of a marriage partner, in the colleagues they have had to work with, in the opportunities they have had for satisfying work, interests and activities. A psychoneurosis can lie latent in a person, embedded as a possibility in his unconscious psychic make-up, and may continue to be dormant in the absence of environmental stress strong enough to disturb his existing ego-defences.

On the other hand, it is equally possible to find many people whose psychic instability undermines what otherwise would be a good marital, vocational or social situation. There is no certainty about the therapeutic operation of real life factors. It is a function of two variables, the degree of instability in the person and the degree of goodness in the environment. We have, therefore, to make a distinction between supportive psychotherapy and radical curative psychotherapy. Once definite breakdown has occurred, perhaps we should say that the older a person is the more we are forced to avail ourselves of the resources of supportive therapy; since the mind grows less resilient for fundamental change as age advances, and the incentives for undergoing the painful process of radical re-development are not so powerful as they are with a younger person who has the greater part of life still in the future. The younger the patient is, the more worthwhile it is to seek radical treatment. Yet we cannot be dogmatic for even this generalization is affected by the differences between individuals. There are some older people who are less rigid and more open to change than some younger ones.

The distinction between supportive and radical curative psychotherapy is much easier to make in theory than in practice. There are certainly cases where the finding of a good friend stabilizes a person more dramatically and even permanently than a long psychoanalytical treatment would. Yet there are other cases where excellent friendships or engagements to marry are repeatedly broken off owing to the 'difficult' behaviour of the neurotic individual. *In some cases friendship or marriage is psychotherapeutic, in others psychotherapy is needed to enable a person to succeed in friendships and marriage. The same must be said about religion.* In some cases a religious experience stabilizes a profoundly disturbed person, as can be seen from the lives of such men as John Bunyan, George Fox, Jeremiah and St. Paul. In other cases a person has to sustain his religious faith and experience in the face of continuing psychic disturbances as with the badly depressed Luther. In yet other cases, severe psychoneurosis adulterates religious experience, reducing it to exceedingly immature and neurotic forms.

Thus we are compelled to distinguish between psychotherapeutic agencies or procedures which are primarily supportive to the conscious ego and the therapy which seeks to change the deep unconscious sources of personality disturbance. It is, in fact, a question every psychotherapist has to decide with regard to his patients: shall we support and strengthen the conscious self or probe into the unconscious depths, shall we reinforce repression or open up the repressed? The answer can only be given on the merits of each individual case.

The good and helpful relationships of the outer life of the present day have their direct effect in the form of supporting the conscious personality, and strengthening its resistance against the disturbed unconscious parts of the total self. We cannot say that they have no effect on the unconscious at all but it is for the most part indirect. *The life of the present day is the concern of consciousness, the life of the past is the concern of the unconscious.* Our personality make-up and our inner psychic life is the deposit of all our past experience; it *is* the past in so far as that is still alive within us. The more unhappy childhood was, the more, in self-defence, it is excluded from consciousness and kept from interfering with the life of the present day, so far as that is possible. The unconscious, as we have seen, is largely built up and structured by the process of burying and forgetting precisely all that was most difficult and disturbing in early life. It is, therefore, the part of the self which is purposely kept out of direct touch with the consciously apprehended life of the outer world of the present day. It is astonishing to discover, in the analysis of an adult person, how little the unconscious has changed through the years.

In dealing with a patient over fifty, unless there are very good reasons for taking a different course, I usually explain this in a simple way. It is as if the life of the present day is being lived in the front parlour of the mind, while at the same time the life of childhood is still being lived, vividly and disturbingly, in the back kitchen; and a barrier is erected across the passage that connects them. With advancing years the barrier has weakened, but it would be too disturbing and take too long to pull it down and bring out all the troubled early life into consciousness. The patient would simply feel that he was getting worse and worse, not better. It is more sensible to seek to strengthen the barrier again. A plain intellectual explanation of the situation can remove much of the mystery, so long as the conscious ego is not too much undermined. A patient can be helped to accept the legacy of early life in the region of personality as something to be adjusted to, in the same sense as one would have to accept the legacy of poliomyelitis in childhood, say a withered limb, and live in spite of it. It is better to take such a course frankly than to hold out hopes of cure that discourage the patient by not materializing. He can be helped to understand that even his symptoms, phobic reactions, annoying little anxieties about whether doors are locked, taps turned off, etc., compulsions to tidiness, and even some physical symptoms, are intelligible parts of his strategy of defence and means of 'containing' the unconscious, much as an enemy army may be 'contained' and immobilized; the unconscious is treated as a kind of Tobruk in which an army is penned up and sealed off. It is not necessarily wise to seek the removal of these symptoms in advancing years, though actually they may be diminished by understanding their purpose and simply accepting them. In that case it is as well that the patient's family also should be helped to understand the fact that the patient is not just being silly or awkward, but has a real problem of internal emotional disturbance to master.

Where, by reason of age, such a line is taken, it is clear that religion, along with all the patient's other real life interests and convictions, can, and should, play an important part in maintaining the stability of the conscious self against internal threats. But in that case care must be taken to pursue the right course. If the patient is told that if he prays to God, God will cure him, or take away his symptoms or illness, he is being headed into disillusionment. He should be helped to keep his eyes wide open to the fact that his trouble is an unhappy childhood embedded in his personality make-up. It cannot be removed but he can be strengthened over against it. Religion will help in this by being maintained as a live, healthy, all-important concern of his present day existence.

With younger people who become disturbed in their personality, a more radical analytical approach is usually justifiable. It is permissible to use a physical analogy when we are trying to conceive what happens in the case of phenomena not materially visible. We may liken the mind, therefore, to a spatial system divided into parts, and having energy distributed throughout. If we suppose that a certain amount of mental energy is available, then the more of it that is drawn into activity in one part, say the conscious mental life, the less of it will be available to activate other, unconscious areas. If our conscious life in the outer world of the present day is good enough, it will drain mental energy away from the unconscious. That happens in fact every day and night. The activity of the day draws mental energy into our outer life. That diversion ceases at night, and in sleep energy flows back into the inner world, and our past comes alive again in our dreams. An unhappy past may be overshadowed by a happy present.

Fairbairn regards the structural pattern of each individual psyche, conscious and unconscious, as practically unalterable once it is formed, but if libidinal needs find profound satisfactions in real life, then the libidinal pathways to bad internal objects in the unconscious can be drained of energy, and become like dried-up watercourses (*Psycho-Analytic Studies of the Personality*, p. 130). If, however, the individual's circumstances in the everyday world should deteriorate badly, if relationships with real bad objects are forced on him, if tragic accidents or misfortunes befall him or he becomes the victim of injuries at the hands of hostile or unscrupulous people, or finally if illness or old age deprive him of energy or interests, then he may be turned in upon himself, and his available mental energy may flow back into the old patterns again. Dormant conflicts can be reactivated in his unconscious inner world and anxiety states arise. However real the external causes of unhappiness and suffering may be, it is certain that they do not by themselves account for all the anxiety they arouse in us. The external situation meets and excites an internal one, and our waking conscious self is always living between two worlds, the outer and the inner. Here, again, it is evident that in misfortune, illness, and old age, the maintenance of normal interests in the present day and the sustaining of an active religious life are of the greatest importance. So far as religion is concerned, the danger of disillusionment arises only when it is expected that a miraculous cure should be provided. The function of religion here is to maintain faith, courage and determination in facing and resisting difficulties that cannot be removed from the deeper levels of the psychic life.

Psychotherapy in the specialized sense seeks to do something more radical than provide supporting and satisfying experiences for the conscious self, in cases where that promises to be a possibility. It seeks to invade the hidden recesses of the shut-in, unconscious world where all the worst experiences of the past are perpetuated and exaggerated. It seeks to open up that sealed-off inner world in order that the analyst may, as it were, go into it with the patient to rescue the overpowered child from the internalized bad-object aspect of parents by whom his natural vital self-expression was stifled. Psychotherapy seeks to introduce new good object experiences not only into the conscious, but also into the deep and disturbed unconscious life, so as to set the individual free for new developments.

The position as the patient experiences it was made crystal clear by the patient who dreamed that she had to go down dark stairs into the earth (into her unconscious) and was too terrified to go because at the bottom there was a woman (the bad mother) hating a girl child. But she saw me and ran and clasped my hand and said: 'Will you come down with me? I can go if you'll come, but I can't go alone.' The difficulty of breaking into the inner hard core of the repressed unconscious was made plain by a patient who said: 'I feel we've cleared all the outlying areas of my neurosis and I've made useful gains. But now I feel I've come to a circular wall and I can't see over or get through. I don't know what's inside and I'm just going round and round it.' One of his glimpses into that inner region was a dream where he was in a concentration camp being hunted and beaten up by a horde of father figures, his actual father being at their head. In that deepest inner region there lives the persecuted child itself, in the power of, and also under the authority of, adults who overwhelm him. It is in that inner world where he needs to be saved.

It is easy to understand that, in cases where the parents were frankly bad. It is not so easy to understand where the parents by all ordinary standards would be judged to be excellent people. But adults often fail to realize how easily the tender and undeveloped mind of the child can be overawed and frightened by grown-ups who, by comparison, are so big and overpowering. They can obtain a mental ascendency over the child which in many cases is never really thrown off even when hidden and disguised. One patient, a professional man, said: 'I'm coming to feel that my father has such a hold over me that I regard it as impossible to deviate from his opinion. Father was simply always right and never had to be questioned. If he says two and two are three, then they are three. It doesn't matter what you or anyone else says. It doesn't matter that I know they are not. If he says they are, then they have to be.' This irrationality was an emotional truth for him, and he was surprised to find how much his father secretly controlled his emotional reactions to life in spite of the many intellectual differences from his father he had come to adopt.

At times, it seems, that parents can have a positively hypnotic effect on the child which persists as an unconscious factor in their mentality in after years. Many adults report that as children they felt that their parents could see right through them. Fear of a parent's stern and searching eyes is often reported. One very nervous woman stated that she knew her parents loved her and were really kindly people, but her upbringing was strict and the very thought of her mother's loud voice and her father's stern face always made her shrink inside. Parents of strong personality usually do not appreciate the extent of the necessity for them to hold back lest they arouse a sense of helplessness in the small child. Once the child's self-confidence is secure, then definiteness and firm character in the parent is a necessary model for the child's development, but it can easily have the effect of making the child feel ineffective by comparison. One patient who wasted much of his opportunity at school through a deep sense of discouragement about his ability to achieve anything, remembered looking at his father when he was small and thinking: 'I could never be what he is; it's useless to try.'

It is invariable to find that in the unconscious people feel they have no rights against parents to develop an independent individuality of their own. At this point we may take up the question of religion. Religion can be so taught as to emphasize and confirm the deep inner subordination and stifled spontaneity of the vital heart of the personality. It is a common experience in psychotherapy to find patients who fear and hate God, a God who, in the words of Professor J. S. Mackenzie 'is always snooping round after sinners', and who 'becomes an outsize of the threatening parent. That means almost irreparable damage. The child grows up fearing evil rather than loving good; afraid of vice rather than in love with virtue. To the degree the parents elicit guilt-feelings to that degree the child grows up with a feeling of insecurity' (*Nervous Disorders and Character*, 1946, p. 57).

On the other hand religion can be so taught as to protect and preserve the inalienable right of every individual to be his own true and proper self, to grow from within and not merely to be a lump of human clay upon which someone else's pattern has been stamped. One deeply religious patient felt that he had got to go back to his parents (even though they were now both dead) to get their permission to think differently from them and to be himself. I did not hesitate to say: 'You have no need of their permission to be yourself. Their true business was to safeguard your freedom to develop your own nature and to guide you, but not to force all their ideas automatically upon you and make you a replica of themselves. You have the authority of Christ Himself who said: 'Thou shalt love the Lord thy God, and thy neighbour *as thyself*' (Mt. xix, 19).

It is noteworthy that the Old Testament Dispensation of the Law said 'Thou shalt honour thy father and thy mother' (Exod. xx, 12) but no word was said about the parents' responsibility to be worthy to be honoured, and to honour their children. The New Testament Dispensation of Grace shows the Christ of the Gospels speaking in very different, and by comparison very strange, terms. 'I came to set a man at variance against his father, and the daughter against her mother, and the daughter-in-law against her mother-in-law; and a man's foes shall be they of his own household. He that loveth father or mother more than me is not worthy of me' (Mt. x, 35–7). It would be a stupid misunderstanding to regard these words as an incitement to family strife. Christ's solicitude for His own mother on the Cross is sufficient refutation if it should be required. Once when His mother and His brethren came to seek Him while He was teaching, and this was reported to Him by the crowd, He answered: 'Who is my mother? and who are my brethren? And He stretched forth His hand towards His disciples and said, Behold my mother and my brethren. For whosoever shall do the will of my Father which is in heaven, he is my mother, and my sister, and my brother' (Mt. xii, 48–50).

Christ clearly taught that there is no final and absolute authority in the will and ideology of parents, and they have no rights over the child in the face of real values. Christ did not hesitate to transcend family ties, and did not regard them as the ultimate arbiters of the individual's fate and development. Parents are the guardians but not the property owners of the child's personality, and the Christian faith has stood for the innate and eternal value of every individual soul of man. That is not only a charter of freedom against the mass tyranny of the political dictator who would hold the lives of individual human beings cheap, and claim the right to liquidate them at will if they refuse to submit to his pattern. It is equally the charter of freedom that gives every child an unchallenged right to become a true individual in his own right, and not just an enforced copy of his parents.

Human life, moreover, must be seen ultimately in the widest setting. Its significance cannot be exhaustively explained by the scientific analysis of its physical and psychological constitution and of the development of individual human beings. It seems that our very nature compels us to search for the meaning and purpose latent in our existence, and to seek it not only in our relationship with one another, but also in our relationship to the universe itself, to whatever we conceive to be the ultimately real. The present day decline of interest in official religion proves nothing. There are periods of decline and revival in all the major human interests. The practical need to develop a more reliable scientific understanding of our material environment has dominated our civilization for several centuries, and diverted concern away from the more difficult and disturbing problems of man's inner life. It has created, in addition to an astounding expansion of knowledge of a utilitarian kind, many very naïve and simple-minded faiths and hopes. The truly pathetic faith in the power of science and the intellect to save man, to which many fled, has already been extremely rudely shaken. No doubt it will give place in a later age to a rebirth of the major interest in the needs of the heart and the end of existence towards which all our, at present, fevered and anxious activity tends. We have already quoted the view of Professor A. Toynbee that the time is now ripe for a reversal of the seventeenth-century flight from religion to science and technology.

Is religion fantasy and fiction, or is it a real sensitiveness to the larger issues of our existence as human *persons*? This is not the place to discuss this problem, and psychology has no competence to settle the question. There is certainly no place here for dogmatic scepticism, but only for reverent and patient questing for that all-embracing meaning of life that man's very nature has in every age driven him to seek. R. H. Thouless defines religion as 'a felt practical relationship with what is believed in as a superhuman being or beings' (Introd. to *The Psych. of Religion*, p. 4). I would prefer to describe religion as *experiencing a relationship with the ultimate all-embracing reality regarded as personal*. Personal object-relations are the very substance of human living, the matrix of our development as persons and the fact of fundamental significance for the psychology of man. It is plain matter of fact that there is no age in which multitudes of human beings have not sought to experience their relationship to the environing universe on a personal level.

There is no evidence to prove that religion can be dismissed in Freud's manner as the mere 'security-hunger' of immature minds or the 'obsessional neurosis' of guilt-burdened minds. The evidence rather shows that religion is but one of many other major human concerns such as marriage, politics, art, recreation, all of which can be used in that way where the need to do so exists. There is a great deal of immature and neurotic religion, for there is no aspect of human life that neurosis does not touch and disturb. But again, there is no evidence that the more mature a person becomes, the more inevitably he loses interest in these ultimate questions concerning 'man and his place in nature'. The evidence is rather to the contrary. A prosaic, unimaginative and unimpassioned intellectual may dedicate himself narrowly to the scientific and materialistic dissection of phenomena. Mature and sensitive minds will still experience a loving *rapport* with the all-environing reality, and will express this in personal terms as communion with God.

Neither psychology nor any other science can pronounce on the ultimate truth and validity of that experience and belief. We are concerned here with its bearing on psychotherapy and the cure of mental pain. It is a plain matter of fact that the religious experience and faith of a mature person gives the most comprehensive and invulnerable security, and the largest scope for self-realization possible to man. I do not say that that proves the objective truth of religion. I note it as a psychological fact. The best of parents cannot guarantee to us, or enable us to reach, full maturity and peace of mind. They can lay a sound foundation but we still have to erect our own building on it, and to make of life something that is fully meaningful and satisfying to us. They may enable us to orient stably to one another on a finite human plane in our basic emotional relationships, and that will always content many. Nevertheless, life can embrace more than that and the spirit of man does not remain merely earthbound. The fullest maturity involves an adjustment to the whole as well as to its parts. It does not involve any specific theology or philosophy, but it does involve an essentially religious way of experiencing life. The history of religion shows, in fact, that man's religious quest always centres upon the very two basic requirements of psychotherapy. The patient needs to feel, firstly, that his analyst is a reliable protector against the devils and spiritual dangers that haunt him within himself, and, secondly, that as this need subsides the analyst should be found to be providing a good mature personal relationship within which the patient can discover and develop his own proper personality. Religion likewise moves from a quest for *Salvation* towards an experience of *Communion*, in this case with the Ultimate.

Psychotherapy is evidently a truly religious experience and religion at its maturest is the fullest attainment of the aims of psychotherapy. Whether religious experience can penetrate into the unconscious depths of the personality in the way that psychoanalytical psychotherapy can do, is a matter for factual investigation. I would be prepared to say that a sound and enlightened religious faith and some capacity for religious experience in spite of personality disturbances provides the best and most hopeful setting for psychotherapy.

Meanwhile, it behoves the teachers of religion to understand the psychotherapeutic needs of human beings so that religion can be safeguarded against being taught in such a way as to be injurious to mental health; and so that, positively, it can be taught in such a way as to play its full part in maintaining mental health.

Professor Mackenzie attributes to the cultivation of morbid guilt such things as 'rigoristic ethics, the doctrine of eternal punishment, and the penal theories of the Atonement'. By contrast he writes:

'The *enjoyment of God* should be the supreme end of spiritual technique; and it is in that enjoyment of God that we feel not only saved in the Evangelical sense, but safe: we are conscious of belonging to God, and hence are never alone; and, to the degree we have these two, hostile feelings disappear. It is possible to state the same thing in another way. The relationship to God and man, and to our moral ideals should be one of spontaneity. It is not our submission God wants but our spontaneous love and fellowship: a mere submission to moral ideals transforms that which ought to be the outcome of a free and spontaneous choice into a compulsion, and no man is safe whose morality is a compulsion. "Henceforth I call you not servants but friends"; that is the relation between God and man which

spiritual technique should make its supreme aim to culti-
vate. "If you love Me you will keep my commandments";
Christian morality springs out of this spontaneous love
relationship between God and man. In that relationship
Nature seems friendly and homely; even its vast spaces
instead of eliciting a sense of terror speak of the infinite
love; and the nearer beauty becomes the garment with
which the Almighty clothes Himself' (op. cit. pp. 36–7).

For those to whom religion does not represent a real
experience, these words will have little meaning. For those
who do regard religion as a reality, this is the kind of religious
teaching that will promote mental health, and allow religion
to exercise its full psychotherapeutic power.

Bibliography

J. Bowlby. *Child Care and the Growth of Love.* (Baltimore, Pelican Books, 1955.)

M. Brierley. *Trends in Psycho-Analysis.* (London, Hogarth Press, 1951.)

W. R. D. Fairbairn. *Psychoanalytic Studies of the Personality.* (London, Tavistock Publications, 1952.)

H. Guntrip. *Psychology for Ministers and Social Workers.* (Chicago, Allenson, 2nd Ed., 1953.)
———. *You and Your Nerves.* (London, Allen and Unwin, 1952.)

Rollo May. *Man's Search for Himself.* (New York, Norton, 1953.)

Melanie Klein and Joan Riviere. *Love, Hate, and Reparation.* (London, Hogarth Press, 2nd Ed., 1953.)

H. C. Rumke. *The Psychology of Unbelief.* (New York, Macmillan, 1952.)

Clara Thompson. *Psychoanalysis, Evolution, and Development.* (New York, Nelson, 1950.)

L. Weatherhead. *Psychology, Religion and Healing.* (Nashville and New York, Abingdon, 1952.)

Index